Raspberry Pi 3 Mastery - 2 Books in 1

The Raspberry Pi 3 Introductory Book and The Raspberry Pi 3 Project Book - With Source Code and Sep by Step Guides

This book is part of the series:

The Wonderful World of Engineering

Book 1 - Raspberry Pi 3

Setup, Programming and Developing Amazing Projects with Raspberry Pi for Beginners - With Source Code and Sep by Step Guides

This book is part of the series:

The Wonderful World of Engineering

Part I: Getting Started with the Raspberry Pi

The Raspberry Pi is a very common device all over the world. A lot of people young and old are using it to learn to program using of the common programming languages. The device is also widely used for playing computer games. Most Raspberry Pi users don't know that it can be used in multiple ways, including home automation. It will be good to enjoy maximum usage. This book is a guide for you on how to use the Raspberry Pi 3. You are guided from the basic steps of setting up the device to be ready for usage to utilizing to accomplish complex tasks.

If you have just acquired your Raspberry Pi and don't how to use it, this is the best guide. If you have been using a Raspberry Pi for basic tasks and you need to know how to maximize usage, this book will also be good for you. Have you ever wished to know how to program your Raspberry Pi with Python programming language? This book will guide you step by step. The examples given in this book are for Raspberry Pi 3, so ensure that you are using this version of the Pi device. Enjoy reading and enjoy developing!

Chapter 1 - What can I do with the Pi?

The Raspberry Pi is a single-board computer developed to help in teaching the basics of computer science in schools. Several models have been released, with the latest being the Raspberry Pi 3. The device can be applied in a lot of areas and it is commonly used by hackers, artists and students.

The following are a few of the uses of the Raspberry Pi:

1. **Retro gaming**

   The Raspberry Pi can be transformed into a retro game console to play games such as Sega, Nintendo, Arcade and GameBoy. Doing this will not take you more than 30 minutes.

2. **Raspberry Pi tablet**

   The Raspberry device can be transformed into a tablet using the RPi TouchScreen. This can also be done easily and you will get a good result.

3. **Desktop PC**

   You can setup your Raspberry Pi as a useful (although rather slow) desktop computer. However, you will be needed to have other items such as a mouse, screen, keyboard, and if possible, an extra storage device.

4. **Browsing the Web**

   You should also install an operating system available for the RPI such as Raspbian. You will get apps like email for web browsing.

5. **Cloud Server**

   You can transform your Rapberry Pi into a cloud server. You should install a software such as the ownCloud to be able to use the device for storing and accessing files. After setting up your cloud server, you will be able to store your files in your own private cloud storage.

6. **Raspberry Pi Cluster**

   You can build a "supercomputer" from the RPi boards. This is a cool and easy way to learn how to build clusters.

7. **Media Center**

   It is possible to run the media center application for the TV on your Raspberry Pi. This will allow you to organize and play media such as pictures, music, and videos.

8. **Web server**

   You can use your Raspberry pi device as a web server, although a lightweight one. It is capable of handling a small to medium amount of traffic; and you can use it to learn programming languages for the web such as PHP, CSS, HTML and MySQL. You can also use it to launch your own WordPress blog or website.

9. **VPN**

   A VPN (Virtual Private Network) helps you when you need to extend your private network into public places. It is good for a secure and encrypted Internet connection.

10. **PiPhone**

    you can use your Raspberry Pi to build a working phone.

11. **Home Automation System**

    You can create a powerful home automation application from your Raspberry Pi. This can be done by attaching cameras, sensors, relays, and other devices to it. As a result, it will be possible for you to control your home from a remote location. You can add Arduinos to have extra functionalities.

Chapter 2 - How to Setup the Pi

In this chapter, we will be showing you how to setup the Raspberry Pi 3 device. To do the setup, you should have the following:

1. **Raspberry Pi**- make sure you have the Raspberry Pi 3 device.

2. An **HDMI monitor or television**- you will be expected to connect your Pi to a monitor, meaning that an HDMI-enabled screen will be needed.

3. A **USB mouse and keyboard**- these are paramount as they will help you control your Pi. Choose any USB mouse and keyboard.

4. A **card reader and 8GB MicroSD card**- rather than a hard drive, the operating system for the Pi should be installed on a MicroSD card. A card of a minimum of 8GB will be needed.

5. Power supply- a micro USB is usually used to power the Raspberry Pi. There are four ports on the Pi 3, so choose a power supply that can supply at least 2.5A.

Once you have all the above accessories, it will be time for you to get started setting up your Pi 3 device.

Using NOOBS to Install Raspbian OS onto SD Card

You should first install the Raspbian OS on the SD card. This is an indication that you should begin by downloading the operating system onto your computer and using a card reader to transfer it to an SD card.

There are two ways to achieve this. You can choose to do the installation of the Raspbian manually: you will use an external software or the command line tool. You may also choose to download then install NOOBS (New Out of Box Software). The latter is the simplest way to do it, so it's the one we will be using. Follow the steps given below:

6. Place the SD card in the computer or a SD card reader.

7. Download NOOBS. Choose the option for "offline and network install." The version will have Raspbian in the download.

8. The SD card may have to be formatted to support the FAT file format. Find a tutorial that guides you as it is beyond the scope of this book.

9. Extract the contents you have downloaded in a zipped format, then move them to a SD card. Once done, eject the SD card and plug it into your Raspberry Pi 3 device.

You will now be ready, and the rest of the work can be done on the Pi device. It is time for you to connect the monitor.

Connecting the Devices

It is easy to connect your devices to Raspberry Pi 3. However, this process should be done in an orderly manner so that the Pi 3 can recognize all the devices you attach.

You should begin by connecting the HDMI cable to the Raspberry Pi 3 and the monitor, and finally adding the USB devices. For those using an Ethernet cable to establish a connection to a router, just do it.

After you have connected everything, connect the power adapter. Raspberry Pi has no power switch, and it turns on automatically after you have connected it to the power supply.

Setting up the Raspbian

Once you boot up the NOOBS for the first time, it will take a few minutes to format the SD card then setup other things, so you have to give it time. A screen will be displayed asking you to install the operating system, which can be done as follows:

10. Move to the bottom of the screen, then choose the language you want to use as well as the keyboard layout you need based on your location.

11. Click on button next to the Raspbian, then on Install.

You should give the NOOBS time to install the Raspbian OS; it will take about 10 to 20 minutes. Once the process is complete, the system will restart and you will be taken to the desktop, and it is from here that you will be able to perform any necessary configuration. Congratulations, now you have "upgraded" your Raspberry Pi to a Raspbian Pi :-)

Configuring the Raspbian Pi

The Raspbian OS comes with a Start menu from which you can launch the file browser, open applications and everything you may need from your operating system. Begin by setting up a connection to the Wi-Fi network and any Bluetooth devices you may need.

Connecting to the Wi-Fi Network

The process of connecting a Raspbian OS is done in a similar manner as with the other modern operating systems. To connect to a Wi-Fi network, follow the steps below:

12. Move to top right corner of the screen, then click on network icon--the one with two computers.

13. Choose the name of the Wi-Fi to which you need to connect, then type in your password.

If you type the correct password, you will be connected to the Wi-Fi network directly. After setting up the Wi-Fi network, you will be able to use it from both the graphical user interface and the command line.

Connecting Bluetooth Devices

You may have Bluetooth devices such as the mouse and keyboard which you will need to connect to your Pi 3 device. In such a case, you have to pair this device with the Pi. The process is determined by the device you need to connect to your Pi, but the steps are straightforward:

14. Click on Bluetooth icon located on upper right corner of the screen.

15. Click on "Add Device."

16. Identify the device to which you need to connect, then click on it and follow the onscreen instructions to accomplish the pairing.

You must now connect your Raspberry Pi 3 to your Bluetooth device. You can play around with it and start to do what you want.

Chapter 3 - Establishing a Remote Connection

Connect to your Raspberry Pi 3

You can establish a connection to your Pi from a remote location. This becomes useful when you don't have a monitor or there is only a laptop in the house. The following are some of the ways you can establish a remote connection to your Pi:

Using SSH on the Command Line

It is possible for you to establish a connection to the command line of your Pi from your computer by using the SSH (Secure Shell). You will then be able to run any commands from your computer and they will be executed on your Pi. However, you will not be provided with the graphical user interface for the Raspberry Pi.

For those working on a project that doesn't expect you have access to the screen, this is the best approach to establish a connection to your Pi.

Let us discuss how you can connect to your Pi from a Mac OS or Linux computer, or just from another Raspberry Pi; you will not be required to install any additional software.

You should be aware of the IP address of your Raspberry Pi. To know this, open the terminal of the Pi and then run the following command:

```
hostname -I
```

If you are using the device without a screen, you can look for the device list on your router or use the nmap tool.

Now that you know the IP address of your Pi, you can run the following commands from your computer terminal:

```
ssh pi@<IP>
```

Note that in this case, the <IP> should be replaced with the IP address of your Pi. For those who get the "connection timed out" error, you have used the wrong IP address to connect.

If the connection runs successfully, you will see an authenticity/security warning. Type "yes" to continue. The warning should only be seen the first time for you to connect to your Pi via SSH.

In case your Pi has taken an IP address for a device that had been connected to your computer before, you will get a warning and prompted to clear the list of the known devices in your computer. Just follow the instructions and run the ssh command for the second time, which should now run successfully.

You will be prompted to enter the password for your Pi. The default password for the Raspbian is "raspberry." Afterward, the Raspberry Pi prompt will be presented to you, and you will notice that it is the same as the one you see on the Pi.

In case you have setup some other user on your Raspberry Pi, the connection should be done by following similar steps. If the connection runs successfully, you will see the following prompt:

```
pi@raspberrypi ~ $
```

You will then be connected to your Pi and are able to run the commands you need.

X-forwarding

You can choose to forward the X session via SSH, and this will enable you to make use of the graphical user applications by use of the −Y flag. The following demonstrates how this can be done:

```
ssh -Y pi@192.168.160.2
```

For Macs using OS X, the X11 is not provided, so be sure you download and install it.

At this point, you are using the command line tool, but it is possible for you to open the graphical user interface. To demonstrate this, run the following command:

```
idle3 &
```

The command will open editor IDLE for Python in a graphical window. If you type the command

```
scratch &
```

the Scratch will open up for you.

If you need to get more information regarding the ssh command, just type "man ssh" on the terminal.

Allowing SSH Access without a Password

It is possible for you to configure your Pi so that it will allow your computer to connect to it via SSH without the need to provide the password. To achieve this, you will have to generate a SSH key.

First check whether there are keys on your computer that you can use to establish a connection to your Raspberry Pi. You can see such keys by running the following command:

```
ls ~/.ssh
```

If you see files with the name "id_rsa.pub" or "id_dsa.pub," you will be have some keys already setup, so it is possible for you to skip the step for generating the SSH keys. If you want to generate other SSH keys, first delete these keys.

Below is the command you can run to generate the SSH keys.

Make sure that you use a hostname which makes sense like "<YOURNANME>@<YOURDEVICE>". Here is the command:

```
ssh-keygen -t rsa -C nicohsam@pi
```

Comments can be added and enclosed within quotes if there are spaces as shown below:

```
ssh-keygen -t rsa -C "Raspberry Pi #235"
```

Once you type the above command, you will asked to choose the location in which you need to save the key. It is good for you to save the key in the default location, which is /home/pi/.ssh/id_rsa, simply by pressing the Enter key.

You will also be prompted to type a passphrase. This is for security purposes as your key will be useless without this passphrase. This means in case someone else copies your key, it will be impossible for them to impersonate you and gain access to the Pi. If you are prompted, just type the passphrase, then retype it again if prompted, and hit the Enter key.

At this point you should be able to see "id_rsa" and "id_rsa.pub" files in the .ssh directory of the home folder. You must run the following command:

```
ls ~/.ssh
```

In my case, I get the following result:

```
authorized_keys  id_rsa  id_rsa.pub  known_hosts
```

The file "id_rsa" forms the private key. You should keep it in your computer.

The file named "id_rsa.pub" represents your public key. This is the key you should put on to machines to which you are in need of connecting. In case the public and the private keys are matched, the connection will run successfully. You can use the cat command to see the public key on your terminal as shown below:

```
cat ~/.ssh/id_rsa.pub
```

This key should be in the following form:

```
ssh-rsa <LONG STRING OF RANDOM CHARACTERS> nicohsam@pi
```

It is now time for you to copy the key from the computer to the Raspberry Pi. If there is no .ssh directory in your Pi, then you must create one as it will help you do the copying. This can be achieved by running the following command:

```
cd ~
install -d -m 700 ~/.ssh
```

For you to copy the public key to the Raspberry Pi, you must use the command given below to append your public key to the "authorized_keys" file on your Pi. Then send it over the SSH with this command:

```
cat ~/.ssh/id_rsa.pub | ssh <USERNAME>@<IP-ADDRESS> 'cat
>> .ssh/authorized_keys'
```

Note that in this case, you will have to perform authentication using your password. You can then run the "ssh <USER>@<IP-ADDRESS>" command and you will be allowed to establish a connection without being prompted to use a password.

However, you may get the "agent admitted failure to sign using the key" message. In this case, you will have to add DSA and RSA identities to your authentication agent and ssh-agent and execute the command given below:

```
| ssh-add
```

If this fails to work, you will have to run the "rm ~/.ssh/id*" command to delete the keys, then follow the same steps. You can also use the secure copy (scp) command to send the files over SSH.

```
Virtual Network Computing (VNC)
```

Sometimes, working directly with the Pi becomes inconvenient. You may need to work on it from some other device by use of a remote control.

The VNC refers to a graphical desktop system for sharing and it can allow you to exercise control over a computer desktop (running a VNC server) from some other mobile device or computer (running VNC viewer).

The VNC Viewer will be responsible for transmitting keyboard and mouse touch events to the VNC Server, and the return will be getting updates on your screen.

With this, you will be able to see your Raspberry Pi's desktop inside the window of your mobile device or computer. You will be able to exercise control as if you were working on the Pi itself.

VNC Connect from the RealVNC comes included with the Raspbian. It provides you with both the VNC Server and the VNC Viewer. The VNC Server will allow you to control the Raspberry Pi remotely, while the VNC Viewer will allow you to control the desktop computers remotely from your Raspberry Pi if this is what you need.

The VNC Server should be enabled before it can be used. By default, it will give you remote access to your graphical desktop, which is running on the Raspberry Pi, and you will use it as if you are seated adjacent.

It is also possible for you to gain some graphical access to your Raspberry Pi in case it is not running some graphical desktop or it is headless.

Enabling the VNC Server

First ensure that you are using the latest version of the VNC Connect. Run the commands below:

```
sudo apt-get update
sudo apt-get install realvnc-vnc-server realvnc-vnc-viewer
```

These commands will help you update the system. You can then go ahead and enable the server, which can be done from the command line or through the graphical user interface.

To do this via the graphical user interface, first boot your Raspberry Pi 3 to its desktop. Next, navigate through "Menu > Preferences > Raspberry Pi Configuration > Interfaces". Make sure that the VNC has been enabled.

The "raspi-config" will allow you to enable your VNC server via the command line. Fun the following command:

```
sudo raspi-config
```

To enable the VNC server, do the following:

Navigate to the Interfacing Options.

Scroll down then choose "VNC > Yes".

Using the VNC Viewer to Connect to the Raspberry Pi

There are two ways you can connect to your Raspberry Pi. You can use one of them or both, and this will be determined by what is best for you.

Direct Connection

It is always easy to establish a direct connection to your Pi as long you are on the private local network. The connection can be done by use of a wired or wireless network either at home, school, or even an office.

You should begin by discovering the IP address by running the "ifconfig" command. Use the device you will need to use to take control over the Raspberry Pi and download the VNC Viewer.

Open the VNC Viewer, then type in the IP address of your Raspberry Pi.

Cloud Connection

You can use the cloud service of RealVNC for free, provided the remote access is done either for non-commercial or education purposes. Connections to the cloud are usually done in a convenient and encrypted manner from end-to-end. They are highly recommended for those who need to establish a connection to a Raspberry Pi over the Internet. You are not expected to configure either a router or a firewall, and it is not a must to be aware of the IP address of the Raspberry Pi, or give some static one.

Begin by creating your account with RealVNC, which is free. Use the credentials for this account to sign onto the VNC Server of your Raspberry Pi.

Download the VNC Viewer on the device from which you need to take control. You can then use the same credentials to sign in to your VNC Viewer, then click to establish a connection to the Raspberry Pi.

Authentication in VNC Server

To complete the cloud, or even a direct connection, you must perform the authentication in the VNC Server. If you are establishing the connection from a compatible VNC Viewer app and from the RealVNC, provide the username and the password which you normally use to log onto the user account on your Raspberry Pi. These credentials take a default of "pi" and "raspberry."

If you are establishing the connection from the non-RealVNC Viewer app, first you will have to downgrade the authentication scheme of your VNC Server, give a password unique to the VNC Server, and enter it instead. On your Raspberry Pi, launch the dialog for the VNC Server by navigating through "Menu > Options > Security," then click on Authentication dropdown to choose "VNC Password."

Create a Virtual Desktop

For those using a headless Raspberry Pi, or one not connected to a monitor, it is less likely for it to be running a desktop.

With a VNC Server, you can create a desktop, which will give you some graphical remote access when you need it. The virtual desktop can be found in the memory of your Raspberry

Pi. For you to create and establish a connection to the virtual desktop, perform the following:

Open the terminal of your Pi or establish a remote connection with SSH, then run the following command:

```
vncserver
```

An IP address will be printed on the terminal, so take note of this value.

Type the information into the VNC Viewer of the device you need to take control of. If you are in need of destroying your virtual desktop, execute the command below:

```
vncserver -kill :<display-number>
```

Any available connections to your desktop will also be stopped.

Chapter 4 - Turning Raspberry Pi 3 into a Media Center

You can transform your Raspberry Pi3 into a XBMC media center in a few minutes. Begin by assembling all the necessary materials. We will be guiding you how to do this. You should have the following materials:

17. A **Raspberry Pi 3**

    we will be using Model 3 of the Raspberry Pi for setup.

18. A **composite or HDMI video cable**

    this cable will facilitate the connection of your Raspberry Pi to a monitor or television.

19. **8GB Class 10 SD Card and a card reader**.

    If you have a better version of the SD card, you can use it as well. We are using the 8GB size for better performance.

20. **A USB mouse and keyboard**

    Choose any standard USB mouse and keyboard as they will work. Also, feel free to use a wireless keyboard and mouse, but note that you will reconnect them whenever your Raspberry Pi reboots.

21. **An Ethernet cable**

feel free to use any standard one as it will work correctly.

22. **A micro USB power supply**

It will be good for you to get one made specifically to be used with the Raspberry Pi. This will ensure that you don't get into problems. Some chargers for smartphones will work.

23. **A remote control**

You may not need to use a keyboard or a mouse for controlling the media center once it has been setup. In such a case, you should have a remote.

24. **USB hard drive**

This is optional and will help to store your videos if you are not in need of streaming the videos from other computers.

25. **A stereo audio cable, 3.5mm**

This is optional for those using an analog video and there is a need to connect the Raspberry Pi to a set of external speakers and internal ones on the monitor or television. For those using HDMI, feel free to skip this step.

26. **Raspbmc Installer**

This will help you put Raspbmc onto the SD card. Go to the official website for Raspbmc and get it for free.

Let's go

After you are done with what has been discussed in this chapter, you will get an XBMC box capable of playing a 720p video. Follow the steps below:

Begin by putting the Raspbmc on the SD Card

Before you can connect your Raspberry Pi to a TV, you should have the Raspbmc installer already in your SD card. First, plug the SD card into the computer. In the case of Windows users, you can download the installer then run it on the desktop to have the Raspbmc on the SD card. For Linux and Mac users, you will have to run some few extra commands; but they are easy. After you have the installer added to the SD card, unplug it and continue to the next step.

Connect the Raspberry Pi, Install Raspbmc

It is now time for you to connect your Raspberry Pi to the TV. Connect your HDMI cable to the TV, connect the Ethernet cable to the computer, insert the SD card into the Raspberry Pi, then connect the micro of your Micro USB power cable to the wall. After connection, expect it to boot automatically from the SD card, which will start the installation process.

You can now let the installer do its work. This will take only 15 to 25 minutes. Once done, it will reboot your XMBC.

Configuration

Now that your XBMC is up and running, you only need to change a number of settings and you will have everything running correctly. The following are the changes to make:

Resolution- you can find this in "Settings > System > Video Output." If you need to watch videos of 720p resolution, the value for this should be changed to 720p. With this, the system and the menus will feel somewhat snappier.

- Overscan- you can find this in "Settings > System > Video Output > Video Calibration." If the XBMC window is not able to fit on your screen, you will have to change the calibrations for your video so they can fit.

- System Performance Profile- you can find this by navigating through "Programs > Raspbmc Settings > System Configuration." This is a setting for the Raspberry Pi which will make it possible for you to overlock the device. After this, everything will be running smoothly and in the right manner. It will be good to use the "Fast" option which help you speed up everything and the stability will remain fine. The setting for "Super" will give a fast speed, but there is a problem as it will create instability.

- MPEG2 Codec License- you should buy this from Raspberry Pi store, then enable it by navigating through "Programs > Raspbmc Settings > System Configuration." With this setting enabled, you will be able to play the MPEG-2 videos, which are the videos your Pi is unable to play out of box. However, if you don't intend to play these types, feel free to skip this step.

You will then be done with the needed configuration, so you can add some videos to your library, install any necessary add-ons, and customize the setup!

Chapter 5 - Building a Retro Game Console

You can use your Raspberry Pi 3 to make a retro game console in a few minutes. To do this, you should first install the operating system on an SD card then perform some simple file sharing from your PC.

To emulate the old-school video games, you should have two things. You should have game ROMS as well as an emulator for playing them. A ROM refers to a piece of a game which can be found on the device. The emulator should be used for playing the ROM.

The emulator ethics rule requires that one have a physical copy of the game if you are using the ROM. You can also create one from old cartridges.

The Raspberry Pi will automatically boot onto the EmulationStation. The programs runs off the custom SD card named RetroPie which allows you to make use of a controller to choose a game and an emulator without having to touch a mouse or keyboard. Once everything has been setup as expected, you will be able to navigate through the Pi and do everything from the controller.

Other than games, you will also be granted full access to media center software called Kodi. You will need to get into the advanced settings to download it. With this, you will have an all-in-one center for entertainment, running classic games and the media center.

Requirements

In this chapter, you should have the following:

27. **A Raspberry Pi**
    We will be using the Raspberry Pi 3. You will have full compatibility with the game and built-in Bluetooth and Wi-Fi.

28. **A micro USB power supply**

29. **An 8GB Micro SD Card, or a large-size one.**

30. **USB game controllers** (optional)

31. **USB keyboard**
    This will help you perform initial setup and if you need to configure the Wi-Fi.

32. **AV/HDMI, TV/monitor cables**

33. **A Mac/Windows/Linux computer**
    for setting up the SD cards and transferring the ROMS.

Once you have assembled the above components, follow the steps given below:

Install RetroPie on SD Card

Due to the work of the RetroPie, the installation of the emulators on the Raspberry Pi is easy. Follow the steps below:

Download RetroPie Project SD card image for the version of your Raspberry Pi, which should be either the 0/B/B+ or the 2/3. In this chapter, we will be using the version 3.7. However, the sucker might take a long time to perform the download based on the level of server activity.

34. After the download is complete, extract your image to your SD card by following a similar approach for a normal Raspbian image. In the case of Windows users, this is easy when you use the Win32DiskManager. For Mac users, make use of the RPI-sd card builder. For Linux users, you can use the terminal.

35. Once done, unplug the SD card from the computer and put it on your Raspberry Pi.

This is enough for the initial setup. For those planning to use the mouse and the keyboard other than the controller, you are almost done, so you can skip a number of steps and begin to transfer the ROM files.

If you prefer doing a manual installation of the emulators, just go ahead and do this. However, it will take a long time, usually about 9 hours to download and do the complete installation. However, with this method, you will be running the latest version of the emulators and you will be able to choose what needs to be installed.

Start the Raspberry Pi 3

In this step, you should boot your Raspberry Pi 3, then setup the EmulationStation. Plug the keyboard and one of the controllers to your Raspberry Pi 3. Insert the SD card that you had just burned. After some minutes of the automatic setup have elapsed, the Raspberry will boot automatically onto the EmulationStation as well as the interface wrapper, and it will have all your emulators on it. This where you will set the controller up and do a few changes for the system to work well.

Once it boots for the first time, follow the onscreen instructions to setup the controller. For those using a Bluetooth controller, this is the best time to connect it with the USB cable. You can then setup its Bluetooth in next step.

Once done, use your controller to navigate through the RetroPie. The controllers should be able to work with all your emulators as well as on the RetroPie. Other than the control of the basic movement, you will get some Hot Keys which can be used to accomplish certain actions within the game. These include:

- Select+Start: Exit a game

- Select+Left Shoulder: Load

- Select+Right Shoulder: Save

- Select+Right: Input State Slot Increase

- Select+X: RGUI Menu

- Select+Left: Input State Slot Decrease

- Select+B: Reset

All the above keys may not be useful, but it is good for you to know how to quit a game, create, save, as well as how to load a save.

It is also beneficial for you to note that even the RetroPie comes with many emulators; and it will hide the ones which do not have the games already installed. This means that as you scroll the RetroPie for the first time, you will not see emulators. The rest of the emulators will be shown when you are adding the games.

Setup the Wi-Fi

The new RetroPie has a in-built system that can allow you to access all the Raspberry Pi settings and tweak the memory from the EmulationStation. The majority of the settings are for advanced users, but it is wise for you to know how to setup the Wi-Fi.

The following steps will help:

36. Scroll down to option for "Configure WiFi," then tap the "A" button.

37. Choose "Connect to WiFi Network" and select your network. Enter the password and choose okay.

That is the base setup and the place from where you can do other changes. You can go ahead and edit the theme for Retropie, set the controller for Bluetooth, manage the files, etc.

Transfer ROMs from Primary Computer

Our assumption in this section is that you have a number of ROMs on your primary computer which you need to move to the Raspberry Pi 3.

Ensure the Raspberry Pi 3 is on and already connected to the router.

If connected, the RetroPie folder will appear as a shared folder automatically in your network. If this doesn't happen, you can go ahead and load it manually. For Windows users, launch the file manager then type "**retropie**" into folder location. For Mac users, launch the finder then choose "Go > Connect to Server." Type "**smb://retropie,**" then click on Connect.

Now, it will become easy for you to copy the ROMS from your computer to the Pi remotely, so you should not be worried if you need to add more. After you are done with the file transfer, just reboot the Pi.

If you need using a USB Drive having ROMS, go ahead and use it.

Part 2: Projects with The Raspberry Pi & Python

Chapter 6 - Programming with Python on Raspberry Pi 3

The Raspberry Pi is a basic tool that can introduce anyone from anywhere in the world to computer programming. The Linux distribution for Raspberry Pi, which is Raspbian, comes with in-built programming languages and IDLEs, which will can help you get started with programming even after powering on the device for the first time.

Python is a very popular programming language across the world. It is highly supported in web applications, desktops, and other utilities. It is the best language for you to learn especially if you are new to programming.

If you are using the latest version of the Raspbian OS, you are lucky as it comes with in-build tools for Python 3.3 and Python 2.x. The latest version of the Python is Python 3.x.

The Command Line and the IDE

To program with Python in the Raspberry Pi 3, you can choose to use either the Integrated Development Environment (IDE) or the terminal, and this will be determined with what you are comfortable. Python has an IDE named IDLE. In this case, we will be exploring the Python 3 IDLE.

To launch the Python 3 IDLE in Python, you just need to click it as shown below:

This will give you the Python shell and will allow you to work with Python in an interactive manner.

However, you may need to use Python from the terminal of your Raspberry Pi 3. To do this, just open this terminal and type the "python3" command. The Python command line will then be presented from which you will be able to run your Python scripts.

We will now demonstrate how you can interact with this terminal. Just type the following then hit the Enter key:

```
>>> 1+ 3
```

Once you hit the Enter key, you will get the sum of 1 and 3, which is 4. Again, type the following on the command line:

```
name = "John"
print (name)
```

Hit the enter key and you will get the value of name, which is John. The screenshot given below demonstrates:

```
>>> name = "john"
>>> print (name)
john
>>>
```

Write the example given below on the command line:

```
print ("Hello, Raspberry Pi 3 is good")
```

Hit the enter key on the keyboard. You will see the statement within the quotes printed on the terminal as shown below:

```
>>> print ("Hello, Raspberry Pi 3 is good")
Hello, Raspberry Pi 3 is good
>>>
```

Updating Python Packages

Python provides you with packages you can use to accomplish a variety of functionalities in your apps. You must install these packages in your local development environment.

The Raspbian Archives provides you with a few packages. The best way to get the packages is by running the "apt-get" commands as shown below:

```
sudo apt-get update
sudo apt-get install <python-package-name>
```

In the first command given above, we are updating the system to ensure that we can get all the updates available. In the second command, the <python-package-name> should be replaced with the name of the package you need to install in your system.

It is good for you to note that the Raspbian Archives do not provide all the Python packages. In such a case, you should use the Python Pip package management system. A good example is the "requests" package that makes it possible for the Python apps to work with the HTTP call functionality. The following command will help install this package:

```
$ pip3 install requests
```

If you need to see the details for the package we have just installed, just run the following command:

```
$ pip show requests
```

You will see details regarding the package.

GPIO Programming

The Raspberry Pi 3 can be used with other types of hardware for the creation of amazing electronic projects. The Pi 3 device itself provides you with 40 GPIO pins that you can use to interface with other types of hardware. You can receive data from these devices or write to them. This means that with the GPIO pins, it is possible to create apps which can write as well as control devices such as turning them on and off.

For you to be able to program the GPIO pins for your Raspberry Pi, you must use the GPIO python library for the Raspberry Pi. The following command will help you to install this library for the Python 3:

```
sudo apt-get install python3-rpi.gpio
```

The command will install the library so you can use it to create some simple applications. However, it is good for you to know that if you are using the latest version of the Raspbian OS, then this library comes pre-installed. In this case, you only have to update it by running the "sudo apt-get update" command.

Let us give an example demonstrating how this library can be used.

Open your Leafpad text editor, then save the sketch with the name "inputSketch.py." First, add the following statement to the file to import the library:

```
import RPi.GPIO as GPIO
```

Then specify the type of numbering system to be used to create the sketch. This can be done using the following code:

```
#set up the GPIO by use of BCM numbering
GPIO.setmode(GPIO.BCM)
#setup the GPIO by use of Board numbering
GPIO.setmode(GPIO.BOARD)
```

Note that a difference exists between the two types of numbering systems. With the BOARD numbering system, the pins will be used and numbered in the exact way they have been arranged or laid on the board. In the case of the BCM option, the Broadcom SoC numbering system is used. The BCM numbering system is the same for all programming languages, so we will be using it in this example.

Building a Circuit

We now get to the inputs and outputs. We will wire two momentary switches to the GPIO pins, that is, 23 and 24, which on the board are the pins 16 and 18. The switch on the pin 23 has been tied to a 3.3V, while the switch on the pin 24 has been placed on the ground. The reason for this is that the Raspberry Pi has both internal pull-up and the pull-down resistors, and you can specify these during the pin declarations.

You can then set the pins by writing the following:

```
GPIO.setup(23, GPIO.IN, pull_up_down=GPIO.PUD_DOWN)
GPIO.setup(24, GPIO.IN, pull_up_down=GPIO.PUD_UP)
```

With the above code, a pull-down resistor will be enabled on pin 23, while a pull-up resistor will be enabled on pin 24. It is now time for you to check to know whether you are able to read them. What the Pi is doing is looking for some high voltage on the pin 23 and for some low voltage on the pin 24. These should also be kept in a loop so that it can check for the pin voltage constantly.

Change your program to look like this:

```
import RPi.GPIO as GPIO
GPIO.setmode(GPIO.BCM)
GPIO.setup(23, GPIO.IN, pull_up_down = GPIO.PUD_DOWN)
GPIO.setup(24, GPIO.IN, pull_up_down = GPIO.PUD_UP)

while True:
    if(GPIO.input(23) == 1):
        print("Button 1 has been pressed")
    if(GPIO.input(24) == 0):
        print("Button 2 has been pressed")

GPIO.cleanup() #attention!
```

When using loops in Python, the indents are very important, so make sure that you indent your code correctly. If you need to access the GPIO pins, you must run your script using the "sudo" command. The command for running the script is as shown below:

```
sudo python inputSketch.py
```

To end the program, press CTRL+C on your keyboard.

> The command *GPIO.cleanup()* used at the end of the program will be used to reset your pins to normal once you exit the program. If you fail to do this, then your GPIO pins will remain in the state you had set them the last time. However, in our little example, the cleanup code is never executed. Can you see why?

How to clean up correctly

If you are dealing with GPIO in your program, always make sure to call *GPIO.cleanup()* at the end. In the design of our programs, we use what's called an enless loop. You can see it in the code example above. The expression "True" is an always will be true until the end of the universe. So "while True" means, that the loop itself would never stop executing. Only the interrupt we send to the program by pressing CTRL+C kills the program. The problem is, that the program is really "killed", so the code after the while-loop will never be executed. To solve this problem, we introduce a try/except/finally structure like this:

```
import RPi.GPIO as GPIO
GPIO.setmode(GPIO.BCM)
GPIO.setup(23, GPIO.IN, pull_up_down = GPIO.PUD_DOWN)
GPIO.setup(24, GPIO.IN, pull_up_down = GPIO.PUD_UP)

try:
    while True:
        if(GPIO.input(23) == 1):
            print("Button 1 has been pressed")
        if(GPIO.input(24) == 0):
            print("Button 2 has been pressed")
```

```
except KeyboardInterrupt:
    print('User terminated program by pressing CTRL+C')
finally:
    GPIO.cleanup()
```

When the user now presses CTRL+C the execution of the try-block (that contains the while-loop) is stopped and the except-block is being executed. The finally block is being executed in the end.

The cool thing about a finally block is, that whatever exception occurs during the execution of the code in the try-block, the finally block is *always* executed. There are a lot of possible exceptions, much more than just the KeyboardInterrupt exception. But whatever the occurring exception might be, the finally block is always being executed. Therefore, it is the right block to cleanup stuff. And we do that by calling GPIO.cleanup().

You can handle exceptions with the exception block, but you don't have to. It is perfectly fine to omit exception handling in our case and just use the try and finally blocks if we just want to cleanup resources. For the sake of simplicity, we will use just use the *try* and *finally* blocks in our future code examples. The above code without the exception block looks like this:

```
import RPi.GPIO as GPIO
GPIO.setmode(GPIO.BCM)
GPIO.setup(23, GPIO.IN, pull_up_down = GPIO.PUD_DOWN)
GPIO.setup(24, GPIO.IN, pull_up_down = GPIO.PUD_UP)

try:
    while True:
```

```
        if(GPIO.input(23) == 1):
            print("Button 1 has been pressed")
        if(GPIO.input(24) == 0):
            print("Button 2 has been pressed")
finally:
    GPIO.cleanup()
```

The Polling Problem

Our code is working, but it will print a line for every line after the button has been released. If you need to trigger an action or a command one time only, this will be inconvenient.

It is good that the GPIO library comes with a built-in falling-edge and rising-edge function. The rising-edge will be defined when the pin has changed from low to high, but only the change will be detected. The falling-edge represents the moment your pin will change from high to low.

Our code can be changed to reflect this:

```
import RPi.GPIO as GPIO

GPIO.setmode(GPIO.BCM)
GPIO.setup(23, GPIO.IN, pull_up_down = GPIO.PUD_DOWN)
GPIO.setup(24, GPIO.IN, pull_up_down = GPIO.PUD_UP)

try:
    while True:
        GPIO.wait_for_edge(23, GPIO.RISING)
        print("Button 1 has been Pressed")

        GPIO.wait_for_edge(23, GPIO.FALLING)
        print("Button 1 has been Released")

        GPIO.wait_for_edge(24, GPIO.FALLING)
        print("Button 2 Pressed")

        GPIO.wait_for_edge(24, GPIO.RISING)
        print("Button 2 has been Released")
finally:
    GPIO.cleanup()
```

After running the above code, you will notice that the statement will run only after detection of the edge has occurred. The reason for this is because Python waits for the edge to occur before it can move to the other part of the code. Note that we have written our code in a sequential manner, so the edges will occur in the same order we have written them.

Edge detection becomes useful when you need to wait for the input before you can proceed to the next part of the code. However, if you need to trigger a function by using some input device, then you should approach this using the events and callback functions as it is the best approach.

Events and Callback Functions

Suppose you have the camera module for the Raspberry and you need to use it to take a photo once you have pressed the button. However, you want to avoid the situation where your code will pull the button constantly, and you don't want to wait for too long for this to take place.

The use of a callback function gives us the best approach to run this code. The function has been attached to some specific GPIO pin and it will run whenever the edge has been detected. Try this with the following code:

```
import RPi.GPIO as GPIO

GPIO.setmode(GPIO.BCM)
GPIO.setup(23, GPIO.IN, pull_up_down = GPIO.PUD_DOWN)
GPIO.setup(24, GPIO.IN, pull_up_down = GPIO.PUD_UP)

def printFunction(channel):
    print("Button 1 has been pressed!")
    print("Note the way the bouncetime affects a button
press")

try:
    GPIO.add_event_detect(23, GPIO.RISING,
callback=printFunction, bouncetime=300)

    while True:
        GPIO.wait_for_edge(24, GPIO.FALLING)
        print("Button has been 2 Pressed")

        GPIO.wait_for_edge(24, GPIO.RISING)
        print("Button has been 2 Released")
finally:
    GPIO.cleanup()
```

In this case, you will see that the button 1 will provoke the *printFunction* consistently, even as the main loop is waiting for the edge on button 2. The reason is because the callback function is contained in a different thread. Threads are of great importance in programming since they allow things to be done simultaneously without affecting anything in other functions.

When button 1 has been pressed, what will happen in our main loop will not be affected in any way.

Threads are also important; you can remove them as easily as adding them, which is shown below:

```
GPIO.remove_event_detect(23)
```

After, you will be free to add some different functions to the pin.

Adding the Functionality

The Raspberry Pi is not setup for PWM outputs or analog inputs. This is true despite the fact that callback functions are good for GPIO pins. However, since the Pi has both the Tx and Rx pins (pins 8, 10, GPIO 14, 15), communication with Arduino becomes easy.

If you are in need of a project that requires analog sensor input, or some smooth PWM output, you can simply do this by writing commands to serial port to Arduino.

Chapter 7 - Adding Electronics: The LED Project

In this section, we will be showing you how to light a LED.

What you need

Other than the Raspberry Pi, you should have the following:

- A breadboard
- An LED
- 330 ohm resistor
- Two male-female jumper wires

Breadboard

The breadboard will provide you with a way to connect your electronic components and you will not have to solder them together. We use them to test the design of a circuit before we can create a printed circuit board (PCB). The breadboard holes are usually connected in a certain pattern.

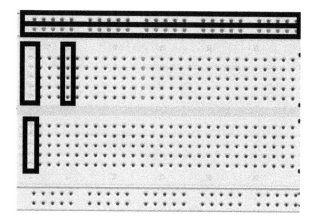

The holes in the top row are connected together. The same applies to the holes in the second row and the last 2 rows of the breadboard.

In the center area, there are 2 blocks of 5 lines of holes each. The holes of each column in each line are connected. In the image above, some of the connected holes are indicated with rectangles to help you get an idea of how it works.

At first, this might seem a bit strange, but actually this setup proves to be very convenient when designing circuits for prototyping.

LED

A LED (Light Emitting Diode) will light when electricity is passed through it.

After selecting a LED, you will realize that there is a leg that is longer than the other one. The longer leg is known as the anode, and it must be connected to the positive supply of your circuit. The shorter leg is known as the cathode and is connected to the negative side.

The LED will only work if you supply power in the correct order. Connecting them in the wrong way will make them fail to light but it will not break them.

The Resistor

Resistors are used when you need to connect your LEDs to the GPIO pins on your Raspberry Pi. Your Raspberry Pi is only capable of supplying a small current of about 60mA.

Note that your LEDs need more power than this, and they can burn your Pi. The purpose of resistors in the circuit is to ensure that only a small amount of current passes and that the Pi is not damaged. In this case, we will be using 300 ohms resistors that can be identified by their color codes.

Jumper wires

These are used on the breadboard to jump from one connection to another. You will be using those having different connectors at their ends.

Building the Circuit

The circuit will be made up of a power supply, which is the Pi, the LED which will light after power is passed, and a resistor for limiting the amount of power flowing in the circuit.

One of the ground pins will be used to act as the 0 or negative ends of the battery. A Gpio pin will provide us with the positive end for our battery. In this case, we will make use of the pin 18. If taken high, meaning the output will be of 3.3 volts, our LED will light. The connection should be done as shown below:

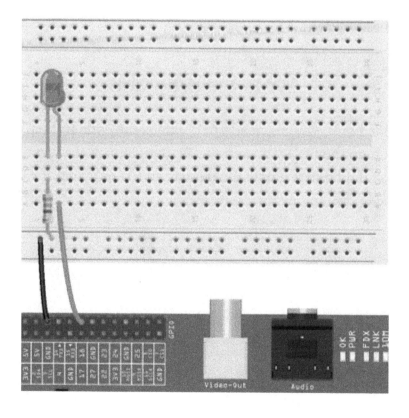

In the next step, just turn off the Pi if you short on something accidentally. You should use one jumper wire to connect the ground pin to the rail, which is marked with blue on the breadboard. The corresponding female end should then go to the pin of the Pi, while the male one to a hole on your breadboard.

The resistor should then be connected to the same row on the breadboard to a column.

The LED legs should then be pushed to the breadboard, while ensuring that the right leg is on the right. You can then complete the circuit by doing a connection of pin 18 to right your LED's right side leg.

Write the program

At this point, you are ready to create some code to help you switch on the LED. Turn on the Pi, then launch the terminal. You should create a new file named ""LED.py." Just type the following command on the terminal:

```
nano LED.py
```

Add the code given below to this file:

```
import RPi.GPIO as GPIO
import time

GPIO.setmode(GPIO.BCM)
GPIO.setwarnings(False)
GPIO.setup(18,GPIO.OUT)

print "LED is on"
GPIO.output(18,GPIO.HIGH)
```

```
time.sleep(1)

print "LED is off"
GPIO.output(18,GPIO.LOW)
```

After the code has been typed and checked, save and then exit the text editor by pressing "Ctrl + x" then "y," then hit the Enter key.

To run the code in the file, type the following command on the terminal:

```
sudo python LED.py
```

You should observe how the LED behaves. You will see it turn on for a second and it will then go off. In case you get an error, know that you have an error in your code, so open it in the anno text editor by running the command "nano LED.py," then edit it.

The "import RPi.GPIO as GPIO" statement helps to import the Raspberry GPIO library to our code as we want to use it. We are in need of pausing our script. This is why we have used the "import time" to import the "time" library which will help us achieve this.

We are also using different names for our pins. The "GPIO.setmode(GPIO.BCM)" statement will help the Python interpreter know the kind of numbering system we are using. The "GPIO.setwarnings(False)" statement helps us turn off the feature for printing warning messages on the screen.

The "GPIO.setup(18,GPIO.OUT)" statement has been used to tell the interpreter that pin at number 18 will be used for the purpose of displaying information.

The statement "print "LED is on" has been used to help print a message the screen. The Statement "GPIO.output(18,GPIO.HIGH)" helps turn on our GPIO pin. This is an indication that our pin has been made to provide a power of 3.3 volts. This voltage is enough to turn the LED on. The "time.sleep(1)" will help us pause the Python program for a second. The next line is simple as it helps print some information on the screen.

The statement "GPIO.output(18,GPIO.LOW)" helps to turn off our GPIO pin, which is an indication that it will no longer be supplying power.

At this point, you have achieved your target, which is to turn your LED on and off. Congratulations! With Python and Raspberry, you can enhance the functionality of your Pi device.

Chapter 8 - Creating a Photo Frame

The Photo Frame is a good way for you to view the photos of your loved ones or anything which you may need to show on a display. In this chapter, we will be creating a digital photo frame.

What you need

You will need the following equipment:

38. Raspberry Pi 3

39. A micro SD card

40. Wi-Fi dongle or ethernet cable

41. USB Drive or external hard drive

42. Screen (touch screen if available)

The following are also needed, but are optional:

43. USB keyboard

44. Raspberry Pi case

45. USB mouse

Setting up your photo frame

We will be using a Raspberry Pi touch screen, but feel free to make use of any screen you have. You only have to connect the Pi 3 to the screen via the HDMI port, DSI port, or by use of a custom HAT.

It is now time for us to setup the software for Photo Frame.

Our first setting will involve preventing the screen from going blank. This calls for us to implement a power setting on our Pi 3.

The feature which makes the screen go off should be changed in the "lightdm.conf" file. Open this file by running the following command:

```
sudo nano /etc/lightdm/lightdm.conf
```

The file will be opened in the nano editor. Identify the [SeatsDefaults] line, then add the following statement just below:

```
xserver-command=X -s 0 -dpms
```

The file should be as shown below:

```
 GNU nano 2.2.6            File: /etc/lightdm/lightdm.conf

SeatDefaults]
server-command=X -s
type=xlocal
xdg-seat=seat0
pam-service=lightdm
pam-autologin-service=lightdm-autologin
pam-greeter-service=lightdm-greeter
xserver-command=X
xserver-layout=
xserver-config=
xserver-allow-tcp=false
xserver-share=true
xserver-hostname=
xserver-display-number=
xdmcp-manager=
xdmcp-port=177
xdmcp-key=
unity-compositor-command=unity-system-compositor
unity-compositor-timeout=60
```

You can then press "ctrl + x" followed by "y" to save and exit the file.

You can reboot the device, and you will observe that you screen will not go off even after 10 minutes of being inactive. The device can be rebooted by executing the command:

```
sudo reboot
```

You may need to set it up to be in a position to drag and drop images into your Pi 3. In such a case, you must setup a network-attached storage. Thus, you will be able to setup s folder that can be found on a local network. It will also be good to setup SSH (Secure Shell) so you can access the device even as the slideshow continues. You don't have an easy way to exit the slideshow unless you choose to turn the device on and off, and you don't have it start automatically.

We will be using the *feh* package to setup the slideshow. It is a cataloguer and an image viewer. This image viewer will not get bogged down even when you have huge GUI dependencies. We are using it because it is lightweight and has no major complications.

Run the following command to install the package:

```
sudo apt-get install feh
```

It is now time to test whether this package is working as expected. You can achieve this by running the command given below. Ensure that you replace the "/media/NICDD1/test" with the directory where you have stored your image. Here is the command:

```
DISPLAY=:0.0 XAUTHORITY=/home/pi/.Xauthority
/usr/bin/feh --quiet --preload --randomize --full-screen
--reload 60 -Y --slideshow-delay 15.0 /media/NICDD1/test
```

We can now make our command to shorter by using some shorter tags as the following demonstrates:

```
DISPLAY=:0.0 XAUTHORITY=/home/pi/.Xauthority
/usr/bin/feh -q -p -Z -F -R  60 -Y -D 15.0
/media/NICDD1/test
```

You will notice that the command line bar will be locked because you have typed a long-running command. To send it to the background, just type the & sign.

We should now go ahead and store it in some a script file. This can be added or even changed later. The file can be made by running the command below:

```
sudo nano /home/pi/picture-frame.sh
```

In this case, we have named the file "picture-frame.sh." You can then add the lines given below to your file:

```
#!/bin/bash
DISPLAY=:0.0 XAUTHORITY=/home/pi/.Xauthority
/usr/bin/feh -q -p -Z -F -R  60 -Y -D 15.0
/media/NICDD1/test
```

It is now time for you to run the script to test whether it is working. Just run the command:

```
bash /home/pi/picture-frame.sh
```

We need to make this script begin to run during boot time. Since you have the SSH enabled, it is possible to access the Pi from a remote location when you are unable to access the screen or the GUI. You should ensure that this has been done before boot time. You can run the following command to open the "rc.local" file:

```
sudo nano /etc/rc.local
```

You can then identify the "exit 0" command add the following commands below:

```
sleep 10
bash /home/picture-frame.sh &
```

If you need to kill the process to access the screen again, just run the following command:

```
sudo pkill feh
```

You should now be able to see a slideshow of your images. In case any errors are experienced, doublecheck the steps and make corrections on any errors made.

Chapter 9 - Installing Magic Mirror on Raspberry Pi 3

Magic Mirror refers to a webpage which runs on the web server in your Raspberry Pi. We will be showing you how to set this up.

What you need

You should have the following:

46. Raspberry Pi 3

47. USB mouse

48. A 2A Raspberry Pi power supply

49. Raspberry Pi 3 case

50. MicroSD card reader

51. MicroSD card, 32GB

52. HDMI cable

Hands on

You should have installed Raspbian OS in your Pi, which will allow us to run both Jasper and MagicMirror. Raspbian Jessy is the best for the purposes of this chapter. You can get its image from the archives then burn it to your SD card.

Boot the Pi

Now that you have OS on the SD card, unplug it from the computer and plug it to the Raspberry Pi. Connect the mouse, Wifi USB adapter, keyboard, HDMI cable, and the power cable for your Pi. If you are taken to the shell rather than to the command line, just type the following command to be taken to the GUI:

```
startx
```

The MagicMirror expects that your Pi is Wifi-enabled so that connection to the Internet may be possible and remote access to it.

Click on the network icon located on top right corner of the screen, choose your Wi-Fi, then type in the password and click Ok.

Remote Connection

You can now establish a remote connection to your Pi from your computer. Launch the terminal or the command prompt from either Mac or Windows and type the following command:

```
ssh pi@your-pis-ip-address
```

If you are asked to enter the password, type the default password for your Raspberry Pi.

Configure the Raspbian

It is always good to change the default password for your Pi. Type the following command, then hit the Enter key:

```
passwd
```

The filesystem of your Pi should be expanded so that it can fill all of the available space and boot into the GUI. Again, type the following command, then hit the Enter key:

```
sudo raspi-config
```

Choose Expand FileSystem and press the Enter key.

In the next step, we will our Pi to boot into Raspbian GUI for the Chromium kiosk mode. To do this, choose Enable Boot to Desktop Scratch, then select Desktop Log In. Highlight the choice and use the Tab to get to then hit the Enter key.

Tab over to, hit Enter and reboot your Pi by running the command
below:

```
sudo reboot
```

You can run the commands given below to update the Pi:

```
sudo apt-get update
sudo apt-get upgrade -yes
```

Install Chromium

Chromium is simply a web browser that we will be configuring to run it as a kiosk, as it will provide the interface for Magic Mirror.

It is now time for us to download and install the necessary packages. If you are using the Wheezy version, run the following command:

```
sudo apt-get install chromium x11-xserver-utils
unclutter
```

For those using the Jessle version, run the following commands:

```
wget http://ftp.us.debian.org/debian/pool/main/libg/libgcrypt11/libgcrypt11_1.5.0-5+deb7u3_armhf.deb

wget http://launchpadlibrarian.net/218525709/chromium-browser_45.0.2454.85-0ubuntu0.14.04.1.1097_armhf.deb

wget http://launchpadlibrarian.net/218525711/chromium-codecs-ffmpeg-extra_45.0.2454.85-0ubuntu0.14.04.1.1097_armhf.deb

sudo dpkg -i libgcrypt11_1.5.0-5+deb7u3_armhf.deb

sudo dpkg -i chromium-codecs-ffmpeg-extra_45.0.2454.85-0ubuntu0.14.04.1.1097_armhf.deb

sudo dpkg -i chromium-browser_45.0.2454.85-0ubuntu0.14.04.1.1097_armhf.deb
```

The commands will install all the necessary packages for you.

Installing Apache

The dashboard for Magic Mirror is a webpage, so a web server is needed to host the dashboard. This calls for us to install the Apache server by running the following command:

```
sudo apt-get install apache2 apache2-doc apache2-utils
```

The following command will help you add the support for PHP:

```
sudo apt-get install libapache2-mod-php5 php5 php-pear php5-xcache
```

Restart your Pi for the changes to take effect:

```
sudo reboot
```

After the Pi reboots, the changes made will take effect.

Installing the Interface

There are several dashboards that can be used for Magic Mirror. However, we only need one, so let's go ahead and install it.

Change to the webroot directory:

```
cd /var/www
```

In the case of Jessie, the web root can be the "/var/www/html."

We can then clone the MichMich's MagicMirror repository. The following command will help achieve this:

```
sudo git clone
https://github.com/MichMich/MagicMirror.git
```

This will give us the dashboard that we will be using. You can move files to webroot then remove the old ones as demonstrated below:

```
cd MagicMirror
sudo mv * ..
cd ..
sudo rm -rf MagicMirror
```

At this point, it is possible to open the IP address of your PI on the computer's browser, and you will see the dashboard for MagicMirror.

Customizing the Interface

We can now configure the interface to meet our needs. You only have to open the following file in text editor:

```
sudo nano js/config.js           .
```

You should then change the language from the top to reflect your language. I will be using English:

```
lang: 'en',
Updating Weather Settings
```

The weather settings should be changed to reflect your location (weather.params.q), language (weather.params.lang), and preferred unit (weather.params.units). My configuration is as shown below:

```
params: {
    q: 'Tampa,Florida',
```

```
    units: 'imperial',
    lang: 'en',
    APPID: 'THE_FREE_OPENWEATHER_API_KEY'
}
```

Open the URL http://openweathermap.org/appid on your browser to generate a free API key, then paste it.

MagicMirror also spins on a number of complements determined by the time of the day. The complements can be changed to something else if there is a need .

MagicMirror will also show the default public iCal calendar that shows soccer or football matches. Changes can be made by pasting the public URL of the calendar. After you are finished with the configuration, just save it and exit.

Run Chromium in Kiosk Mode

At this step, we will be configuring chromium so it can run in Kiosk mode. Launch autostart config file in your Nano editor. The config file for wheezy should be opened using the following command:

```
sudo nano /etc/xdg/lxsession/LXDE-pi/autostart
```

For the case of Jessie, this should be done as shown below:

```
sudo nano ~/.config/lxsession/LXDE-pi/autostart
```

It is also good to disable the screensaver. In both Wheezy and Jessie, you only must add the hash (#) symbol to the beginning of the following statement, as shown below, as a way of commenting it:

```
# @xscreensaver -no-splash
```

Our aim is to have the Chromium startup while in Kiosk mode. If you are using Wheezy, add the lines given below to the bottom of the file:

```
@xset s off
@xset -dpms
@xset s noblank
@unclutter -idle 1
/usr/bin/chromium --kiosk --ignore-certificate-errors --
disable-restore-session-state "http://localhost"
```

For Jessie users, add the lines below to the bottom of the file:

```
@xset s off
@xset -dpms
@xset s noblank
@unclutter -idle 1
@chromium-browser --incognito --kiosk http://localhost/
```

To exit the file, just press Ctrl-x, type y, then hit enter key. We should go ahead and modify the BIOS settings for our Pi.

Run the following command to open the BIOS configuration settings:

```
sudo nano /boot/config.txt
```

The display should be rotated for 90 degrees. This can be accomplished by adding the line given below:

```
display_rotate=1
```

If you need to rotate for 270 degrees in the other direction, add the following line:

```
display_rotate=3
```

Enabling HDML Hotplugging

To enable this, identify the following line and then uncomment by removing the hash (#) symbol before it:

```
hdmi_force_hotplug=1
```

Just save then exit the file, and reboot your Pi for the changes to take effect.

```
sudo reboot
```

At this point, the setup for MagicMirror is working, and it will be good for you to create backup for the SD card. Although this is optional, it is wise in any case something negative occurs during the installation of Jasper; and it will be possible for you to revert.

Chapter 10 - Adding Voice Control to Raspberry Pi

This will be done using Jasper. It is an open-source and voice-controlled platform that runs on many systems including the Raspberry Pi. You can use Jasper to build an application that can be controlled by voice for adding things to the Google Calendar, playing Spotify playlists, and even automating your entire home.

In this chapter, we will help you setup Jasper on your Raspberry Pi 3 and enable it to make commands to do things.

What you need

Ensure you have the following:

53. Ethernet cable

54. USB microphone

55. Raspberry Pi 3

56. MicroSD card, 32GB

57. MicroSD card reader

58. Stereo speakers

59. 2A Raspberry Pi power supply

60. Raspberry Pi 3 case

Ensure that your Raspberry Pi 3 is setup with everything, including the Raspbian OS. Establish a remote connection via SSH.

Installing Jasper

For the users of Raspbian Jessie, you are provided with three options on installing the Jasper. These include manual, use of a disk image, and use of an install script.

Let us use an install script to setup this. Use the following command to obtain the Jasper for the Jessie install script:

```
cd ~/
wget https://raw.githubusercontent.com/Howchoo/raspi-
helpers/master/scripts/jasper-installer.sh
```

The script has the name "jasper-installer.sh." You can then use the **sudo** command to run your install script as shown below:

```
sudo chmod +x jasper-installer.sh
sudo ./jasper-installer.sh
```

Note that we first created an executable of the file, and we then executed it in the above command. You will see a message welcoming you to the script. You will be prompted to select STT support, which can be Network or Local. If you are sure your Pi will be connected to the Internet at all times, then choose Network; otherwise, choose Local. In my case, I will choose Network.

Set up the network

The installation pf dependencies will begin, which can take some time, so be patient.

You may get the error given below:

```
Could not open requirements file: [Errno 2] No such file
or directory: '/root/jasper/client/requirements.txt'
```

Troubleshoot this by running the following commands:

```
sudo chmod +x ~/jasper/client/requirements.txt
sudo pip install --upgrade -r
~/jasper/client/requirements.txt
```

The commands will work by reading the required packages for Jasper from requirements.txt and then upgrade/install them as expected.

Creating Jasper User File

It is now time for us to set up the Jasper user profile. The information provided in this case will help us set up various integrations, the localization results, and other things. Change your directory, then create the file by running the following commands:

```
cd ~/jasper/client
python populate.py
```

Type in the profile information you need, which can be first name, last name, phone number, email address, time zone, etc. The profile will be used in specific add-ons that will provide data such as weather, text message alerts, email notifications, and more. You should then choose whether you will receive the notifications via email or text.

You may be prompted to choose the Speech to Text (STT) engine you would like to use. PocketSphinx is the best for you, so you only need to enter the following command and hit Enter:

```
sphinx
```

Run Jasper

You can type the command given below to run Jasper:

```
python /usr/local/lib/jasper/jasper.py
```

Note that Raspbian might have been installed in a different directory; if you get a "not found" message, try the following:

```
python /home/pi/jasper/jasper.py
```

To make Jasper start during startup, use the following:

```
crontab -e
```

Note that we have used cron, used for job scheduling, you can then add the following line of code:

```
@reboot python /usr/local/lib/jasper/jasper.py;
```

Save your file, exit it, then reboot by running the command below:

```
sudo reboot
```

Afterward, you will be able to issue commands to your Jasper and it will respond to them accordingly.

Troubleshooting

You may get an error related to the one given below:

```
RuntimeError: hmm_dir
'/usr/local/share/pocketsphinx/model/hmm/en_US/hub4wsj_s
c_8k' does not exist! Please make sure that you have set
the correct hmm_dir in your profile.
```

In this case, you only must open the "stt.py" file by running the following command:

```
vim /usr/local/lib/jasper/client/stt.py
```

The file will be opened in Vim text editor. Look for the following line:

```
    def __init__(self, vocabulary,
hmm_dir="/usr/local/share/" +

"pocketsphinx/model/hmm/en_US/hub4wsj_sc_8k"):
```

You can then change the line to the following:

```
    def __init__(self, vocabulary, hmm_dir="/usr/share/"
+

"pocketsphinx/model/hmm/en_US/hub4wsj_sc_8k"):
```

Note that the change involves only removing the word "local."

Conclusion

We have come to end of this guide. The Raspberry Pi 3 is a great device, and you can do a lot with it. You can use the Raspberry Pi 3 as a media server, and you can play music with it. You can also use it to run your images or pictures in the form of a slide show. The beneficial aspect of the Raspberry Pi 3 is that it can be programmed with common programming languages such as Python. For instance, you can program its GPIO pins to help you switch the LEDs on and off.

Thank you!

Thank you for buying this book. If you enjoyed reading this text and developing all the fun projects, then I'd like to ask you for a favor. **Would you be kind enough to leave a review on Amazon?**
It'd be greatly appreciated!

All my best wishes,

Steve

Book 2 - Raspberry Pi 3: The Project Book

by
Steve McCarthy

Introduction

This book is a guide for how to create different types of projects with the Raspberry Pi 3. It takes you through the steps to install and use OpenCV (Open Source Computer Vision Library). This is a computer vision library created to provide a uniform platform for computer applications in need of vision capabilities. You will be using this library in a number of projects. The projects in this book have mostly been using either **Python** of **Node.js** for the programming part (but you will also find a bit of **C**, and of course **Bash/Shell Script**). You are guided on how to create a surveillance camera using the Raspberry Pi. You can use it to survey your home for security purposes. The book explains how one can create a photo taker controlled by GPS. This app takes photos automatically once you reach the destinations you will personally specify. You will also come to understand how to use the Google Home and Raspberry Pi 3 together for home automation. You will also learn how to build your own Smart TV using the Raspberry Pi 3. The book helps you create an app capable of face detection using the Raspberry Pi and the Raspberry Pi camera module. You will also know how to create a print server that can be used via the network without having to migrate it from one place to another. If you don't know how to create a weather app with the Raspberry Pi, this book will help you do this.

Prerequisites

This book is a collection of practical and fun projects for the Raspberry Pi. A basic understanding of how Raspberry Pi works and how you can set it up is required to follow the contents. But don't worry if you are totally new to the world of the Pi: I have included "Chapter 0" to provide you with step-by-step instructions to set up your new microcomputer and use it for the projects discussed in the book.

If you are totally new to the Raspberry Pi, I recommend you to check out my book, *"Raspberry Pi - Essential Step by Step Beginner's Guide with Cool Projects and Programming Examples in Python,"* that covers many more basics than the introductory chapter found in this book.

https://www.amazon.de/Raspberry-Programming-Developing-Beginners-Engineering/dp/1546685618

Chapter 0 - How to Set up the Pi

In this chapter, we will be showing you how to setup the Raspberry Pi 3 device. For the setup, you should have the following:

1. **Raspberry Pi**- make sure you have the Raspberry Pi 3 device.

2. An **HDMI monitor or television**- you will be expected to connect your Pi to a monitor, meaning that an HDMI-enabled screen will be needed.

3. A **USB mouse and keyboard**- these are paramount as they will help you control your Pi. Choose any USB mouse and keyboard.

4. A **card reader and 8GB MicroSD card**- rather than a hard drive, the operating system for the Pi should be installed on a MicroSD card. A card of a minimum of 8GB will be needed.

5. Power supply- a micro USB is usually used to power the Raspberry Pi. There are four ports on the Pi 3, so choose a power supply that can supply at least 2.5A.

Once you have all the above accessories, it will be time for you to get started setting up your Pi 3 device.

Using NOOBS to Install Raspbian OS onto an SD Card

You should first install the Raspbian OS on an SD card. This is an indication to begin downloading the operating system onto your computer, using a card reader to transfer it to an SD card.

There are two ways to achieve this. You can choose to do the installation of the Raspbian manually using external software or the command line tool. You may also choose to download and install NOOBS (New Out of Box Software). The latter is the simplest way to do it, and it's the one we will be using. Follow the steps given below:

1. Place the SD card in the computer or an SD card reader.

2. Download NOOBS. Choose the option for "offline and network install." This version will have Raspbian in the download.
    https://www.raspberrypi.org/downloads/noobs/

3. The SD card may have to be formatted to support the FAT file format. Find a tutorial to guide you as it is beyond the scope of this book.

4. Extract the contents you have downloaded in a zipped format, then move them to an SD card. Once done, eject the SD card and plug it into your Raspberry Pi 3

device.

You will now be ready, and the rest of the work can be done on the Pi device. It is time to connect the monitor.

Connecting the Devices

It is easy to connect your devices to the Raspberry Pi 3. However, this process should be done in an orderly manner so that the Pi 3 can recognize all the devices you attach.

You should begin by connecting the HDMI cable to the Raspberry Pi 3 and the monitor, and finally adding the USB devices. For those using an Ethernet cable to establish a connection to a router, just do it.

After you have connected everything, connect the power adapter. Raspberry Pi has no power switch; it turns on automatically after you have connected it to the power supply.

Setting up the Raspbian

Once you boot up the NOOBS for the first time, it will take a few minutes to format the SD card and then setup other things, so you have to give it time. A screen will be displayed asking you to install the operating system, which can be done as follows:

1. Move to the bottom of the screen, then choose the language you want to use as well as the keyboard layout you need based on your location.

2. Click on button next to the Raspbian, then on Install.

You should give the NOOBS time to install the Raspbian OS; it will take about 10 to 20 minutes. Once the process is complete, the system will restart and you will be taken to the desktop; and it is from here that you will be able to perform any necessary configuration. Congratulations, now you have "upgraded" your Raspberry Pi to a Raspbian Pi :-)

Configuring the Raspbian Pi

The Raspbian OS comes with a Start menu from which you can launch the file browser, open applications and everything you may need from your operating system. Begin by setting up a connection to a Wi-Fi network and any Bluetooth devices you may need.

Connecting to the Wi-Fi Network

The process of connecting a Raspbian OS is done in a similar manner as with other modern operating systems. To connect to a Wi-Fi network, follow the steps below:

1. Move to the top right corner of the screen, then click on network icon--the one with two computers.

2. Choose the name of the Wi-Fi to which you need to connect, then type in your password.

If you type the correct password, you will be connected to the Wi-Fi network directly. After setting up the Wi-Fi network, you will be able to use it from both the graphical user interface and the command line.

Connecting Bluetooth Devices

You may have Bluetooth devices such as a mouse and keyboard which you will need to connect to your Pi 3 device. In such a case, you have to pair this device with the Pi. The process is determined by the device you need to connect to your Pi, but the steps are straightforward:

1. Click on the Bluetooth icon located on upper right corner of the screen.

2. Click on "Add Device."

3. Identify the device to which you need to connect, then click on it and follow the onscreen instructions to accomplish the pairing.

You must now connect your Raspberry Pi 3 to your Bluetooth device. You can play around with it and start to do what you want.

That's it for the introduction. Now let's move on to the fun part: the projects!

Chapter 1- Installing OpenCV 3

In this chapter, we will be showing you how to install and have the OpenCV 3 running on your Raspberry Pi 3. Our assumption is that you have your Raspberry Pi 3 already installed with the Raspbian Jessie. Also, ensure that you have access to the Raspberry Pi 3 terminal, either physically or from a remote location.

For those who have ever installed OpenCV on any platform, you must be aware that there are so many dependencies and pre-requisites needed and it can be time consuming.

Let us get started with the installation process:

Expanding the Filesystem

If you have just installed the Raspbian Jessie, your first step should be to expand its filesystem so that it can occupy all the space available on the Micro-SD card. Run the following command:

```
$ sudo raspi-config
```

A new window will pop up asking you to choose an action from the available options. Choose the first option, which is "1. Expand File System" by hitting the enter key on your keyboard. Use the down arrow key to move to the <Finish> button to reboot the Pi by running the following command:

```
$ sudo reboot
```

After the reboot, the filesystem should have been expanded to include all the space available on the Micro-SD card. To verify whether this has happened, you only have to run the "df –h" command.

A number of gigabytes are needed during the compile time for the OpenCV and its dependencies. This means that we should free up some space on the Pi by deleting the Wolfram engine. Just run the following command:

```
$ sudo apt-get purge wolfram-engine
```

Once the wolfram engine has been removed, you will have reclaimed about 700mb.

Installing the Dependencies

First, update and upgrade the already existing packages. Run the following commands:

```
$ sudo apt-get update
$ sudo apt-get upgrade
```

A number of developer tools should then be installed, including the CMake which will help in the configuration of the OpenCV build process. Run the following command:

```
$ sudo apt-get install build-essential cmake pkg-config
```

We can then install a number of image I/O packages that will make it possible to load a number of image file formats from the disk. Such file formats will include TIFF, JPEG, PNG, etc. Run the following command:

```
$ sudo apt-get install libjpeg-dev libtiff5-dev libjasper-
dev libpng12-dev
```

Video I/O packages will also be needed. Such packages will help us load video files of various formats from the disk during streaming. Install them by running the following command:

```
$ sudo apt-get install libavcodec-dev libavformat-dev
libswscale-dev libv4l-dev
$ sudo apt-get install libxvidcore-dev libx264-dev
```

The openCV library has a module named "highgui" used for the display of images on the screen as well as for building some basic GUIs. For this module to be compiled, we should first install GTK development library as follows:

```
$ sudo apt-get install libgtk2.0-dev
```

We can optimize majority of operations inside the OpenCV by installing other dependencies. This can be done as follows:

```
$ sudo apt-get install libatlas-base-dev gfortran
```

The libraries are good for the optimization of devices that are constrained, like the Raspberry Pi.

We also need to be able to compile our OpenCV with Python bindings. This calls for us to install either Python 2.7 or Python 3 header files, as shown below:

```
$ sudo apt-get install python2.7-dev python3-dev
```

If you skip this step, you will encounter errors later on.

Downloading OpenCV Source Code

After setting everything up, we can go ahead and get the OpenCV archive from the OpenCV repository. After getting the archive, make sure you unzip it. The following commands will help you download and unzip the file:

```
$ cd ~
$ wget -O opencv.zip
https://github.com/Itseez/opencv/archive/3.1.0.zip
$ unzip opencv.zip
```

Our aim is to have full installation of the OpenCV 3, which means that we should also get the opencv-contrib as shown below:

```
$ wget -O opencv_contrib.zip
https://github.com/Itseez/opencv_contrib/archive/3.1.0.zip
$ unzip opencv_contrib.zip
```

Note that it is good for you to ensure you get the same versions for the OpenCV and opencv-contrib. If you fail to ensure this, you will get an error during the compile or run time.

Before we can compile the OpenCV just downloaded, we should first install "pip", a Python package manager. This can be done as follows:

```
$ wget https://bootstrap.pypa.io/get-pip.py
$ sudo python get-pip.py
```

If you need to keep the various dependencies in separate places, you can use the concept of virtual environment. You can achieve this by installing the following two packages:

```
$ sudo pip install virtualenv virtualenvwrapper
$ sudo rm -rf ~/.cache/pip
```

Now that you have installed the above two packages, you should update the "~/.profile" file to include the lines given below at the bottom:

```
# virtualenv and virtualenvwrapper
export WORKON_HOME=$HOME/.virtualenvs
source /usr/local/bin/virtualenvwrapper.sh
```

Note that you can use any text editor of choice to do the above. Examples of such editors include the nano, vim and emacs.
Now that you have made changes to the file, you should restart the machine for them to take effect. Also, you can close the current terminal instance and launch another one, or joust logout then log into the system again. You can also achieve this by running the following command:

```
$ source ~/.profile
```

Creating a Virtual Environment for Python

This is the environment that will be used for the computer vision development. Run the following command:

```
$ mkvirtualenv cv -p python2
```

The above command is for users of Python 2.7, and it will help you create a virtual Python environment named "cv". For the users of Python 3, the following command will help you achieve the same:

```
$ mkvirtualenv cv -p python3
```

Thw workon command will then take you to the virtual environment:

```
$ source ~/.profile
$ workon cv
```

To perform a validation and be sure that you are in the cv virtual environment, you will examine the command line; if you see the word "cv" preceding the prompt, then you know that you are in the cv virtual environment. Otherwise, you will not be in the cv virtual environment. To solve this, you will have to run the workon and source commands.

Installing NumPy

You should now be in the cv virtual environment. NumPy is the only package in this case, and it is highly used for numerical processing. Run the following command to install the package:

```
$ pip install numpy
```

Installation will take around 10 minutes.

Compiling and Installing OpenCV

It is now the right time to compile and install the OpenCV. Ensure that you are in the cv virtual environment by double checking the command line. To move to the cv virtual environment, just run the "workon" command as shown below:

```
$ workon cv
```

After you are sure that you are in the cv virtual environment, you can go ahead and make the build by use of CMake as shown below:

```
$ cd ~/opencv-3.1.0/
$ mkdir build
$ cd build
$ cmake -D CMAKE_BUILD_TYPE=RELEASE \
    -D CMAKE_INSTALL_PREFIX=/usr/local \
    -D INSTALL_PYTHON_EXAMPLES=ON \
    -D OPENCV_EXTRA_MODULES_PATH=~/opencv_contrib-
3.1.0/modules \
    -D BUILD_EXAMPLES=ON ..
```

Have a look at the output given above before we can proceed to the compilation step. You can scroll to the section showing the Python version you are using, either Python 2.7 or Python 3, and ensure that valid paths to the libraries, numPy, interpreter and packages have been set properly.

After this, you will be ready to compile the OpenCV. Run the following command:

```
$ make -j4
```

The use of the −j4 command helps control the number of cores which will be leveraged during the compilation of OpenCV 3. Note that we have used a value of 4 because the Raspberry Pi 2 has 4 cores, which will make it compile faster.

However, errors may occur during the compilation due to the use of the many cores. In such a case, it will be good for you to begin the compilation process and use only one core.

```
$ make clean
$ make
```

After a successful compilation, proceed to the next step and install the OpenCV 3 by running the following commands;

```
$ sudo make install
$ sudo ldconfig
```

If you are using Python 2.7 and the OpenCV 3 has installed with no error, the installation should have been done in /usr/local/lib/python2.7/site-packages.
To finish the installation, we should sym-link the bindings of the OpenCV into the cv virtual environment for Python 2.7. The following commands will help achieve this:

```
$ cd ~/.virtualenvs/cv/lib/python2.7/site-packages/
$ ln -s /usr/local/lib/python2.7/site-packages/cv2.so cv2.so
```

In Python 3, the installation of the OpenCV and the Python bindings should be done in /usr/local/lib/python3.4/site-packages. The sym-link can then be done by running the following commands:

```
$ cd ~/.virtualenvs/cv/lib/python3.4/site-packages/
$ ln -s /usr/local/lib/python3.4/site-packages/cv2.so cv2.so
```

At this point, the installation should be done. To test whether everything has run successfully, open a new terminal, run the "workon" and "source" commands, then import Python + OpenCV bindings as shown below:

```
$ source ~/.profile
$ workon cv
$ python
```

```
>>> import cv2
>>> cv2.__version__
'3.1.0'
>>>
```

The OpenCV version should show if the installation is successful.

Chapter 2- Building a Surveillance Camera with the Pi

In this chapter, we will be guiding you how to build a surveillance camera from the Raspberry Pi. The Pi will be recording a HD video once something moves in the area being monitoring. The owner will be able to view a live video on their browser, even with the use of mobile when on the road.
Assemble the following hardware components:

1. Raspberry Pi 3 Model B.

2. Raspberry Pi camera module. It comes with a connector that can be connected to the board.

3. A housing for your camera.

4. Power supply for the Raspberry Pi.

5. SD card.

6. A network connection that will help you connect your Pi to a network.

First, if you don't have the OS installed on your Raspberry Pi, begin by installing it. After the installation, ensure that it is up to date by running the following commands:

```
sudo apt-get install rpi-update
```

```
sudo rpi-update
```

Also, make sure that the packages are updated by running the following commands:

```
sudo apt-get update
sudo apt-get upgrade
```

Establishing a Remote Connection

Now that everything has been setup on your Pi, you should connect to it from your computer. Users of the Windows operating system will have to download and install PuTTy on their computers, which will help them connect to the Linux terminal on the Pi. After that, you will not need a monitor or keyboard connected to the Pi device.

Enable Wi-Fi

If you are in need of running a camera by use of a Wi-Fi USB dongle, an additional step will be needed to make the Wi-Fi work on the Pi.

Open the PuTTy on your Windows and then open the network configuration file by running the following command:

```
sudo nano /etc/network/interfaces
```

The file will be opened in the nano editor. Add the lines given below at the bottom of the file.

```
allow-hotplug wlan0
iface wlan0 inet dhcp
wpa-ssid "YOUR NETWORK SSID"
wpa-psk "WIFI PASSWORD"
```

Ensure that you replace the details given above with the SSID and password for the network. Run the following command to reboot the Pi and check whether it is connecting correctly to the network:

```
sudo reboot
```

Assembling the Hardware

It is now time for us to assemble all the hardware components together. This will be determined by the housing you are using. Your camera LED will light up red each time motion is recorded. If you need to turn off this LED, you can add the line below to the /boot/config.txt file:

```
disable_camera_led=1
```

Installation of Motion Detection Software

"Motion" is a good motion detection or surveillance software as it provides multiple configuration options. This software can be installed from the command line by running the following:

```
sudo apt-get install motion
```

A number of packages will be installed during the installation process, so you just have to type "y' for the installation to continue. The available version of the motion software does not have support for the camera module of the Raspberry Pi. This calls for us to download then install a special build will help us use the Raspberry Pi camera module. The following commands will help achieve this:

```
cd /tmp
sudo apt-get install -y libjpeg62 libjpeg62-dev
libavformat53 libavformat-dev libavcodec53 libavcodec-dev
libavutil51 libavutil-dev libc6-dev zlib1g-dev
libmysqlclient18 libmysqlclient-dev libpq5 libpq-dev
wget https://www.dropbox.com/s/xdfcxm5hu71s97d/motion-
mmal.tar.gz
```

The downloaded file should then be unpacked to the /tmp directory:

```
tar zxvf motion-mmal.tar.gz
```

You can then use the downloaded build to update the downloaded motion. The following commands will help you achieve this:

```
sudo mv motion /usr/bin/motion
sudo mv motion-mmalcam.conf /etc/motion.conf
```

The motion daemon should also be enabled for motion to execute always:

```
sudo nano /etc/default/motion
```

The above command will open its configuration file in the nano editor. You can then change the line to the following:

```
start_motion_daemon=yes
```

The official build of the motion software is capable of supporting the Raspberry camera module. If you need to edit the configuration file for the software, run the following command:

```
sudo nano /etc/motion.conf
```

It is your duty to ensure that the right permissions are set. If the motion is installed via SSH by a user logged in as "pi", it will be good for you to give the user named "motion" permission to execute the motion software as a service after a reboot. This can be done as follows:

```
sudo chmod 664 /etc/motion.conf
sudo chmod 755 /usr/bin/motion
sudo touch /tmp/motion.log
sudo chmod 775 /tmp/motion.log
```

You should also ensure that the motion is running in the background in the form of a daemon. Our aim is to store the log file in /tmp. We have to run the following command:

```
logfile /tmp/motion.log
```

We also need to use some high-quality surveillance video. This is why the resolution has been set to 1280x720 as shown below:

```
width 1280
height 720
```

A real time video is not of importance in this case, but 2 pictures per second will be enough for us:

```
framerate 2
```

We need to configure the motion software to record some frames before and after motion in the image is detected. These have been set to 2 in our configuration:

```
pre_capture 2
post_capture 2
```

We need each motion video to take a maximum of 10 minutes only. This can be configured by use of the "max_mpeg_time" configuration option. This option will work well with the motion-mmal build, but in case you get the error "Unknown config option 'max_mpeg_time'", you will have to use the max_movie_time or the motion-mmal build.

```
max_mpeg_time 600
```

A number of video players such as VLC will not be able to play the videos recorded, which is why we have changed the codec to msmpeg4. After that, the movies will play well in all players:

```
ffmpeg_video_codec msmpeg4
```

We also need to access the live stream from anywhere. If we fail to configure this, then only the local host will be able to access the live stream. The following command will help us enable this:

```
stream_localhost off
```

If you are in need of protecting the live stream by use of a username and a password, then you only have to enable the following:

```
stream_auth_method 2
stream_authentication SOMEUSERNAME:SOMEPASSWORD
```

Once the above changes have been made to the motion.conf file, you can reboot the Pi:

```
sudo reboot
```

After the reboot, you will see the red light of your camera go on, which is an indication that the motion is using your camera for motion detection.

Saving the Videos

The SD card of Raspberry Pi has limited space. This is why we will be storing the recorded videos on a Window server.
Begin by sharing a folder or folders from a windows machine. Whether you are accessing the Pi from PuTTy or directly launch the fstab configuration on the Raspberry, execute:

```
sudo nano /etc/fstab
```

An extra line showing the configuration of the Windows network shared folder should be added:

//YOURSERVERNAME/YOURSHAREDFOLDERNAME
/mnt/camshare   cifs
username=YOURSHAREDFOLDERUSERNAME,password=
YOURSHAREDFOLDERPASSWORD,iocharset=utf8,file_m
ode=0777,dir_mode=0777 0 0

Be sure that the user has been granted permissions to save files to your shared folder. After rebooting the Pi, it should have the folder /mnt/Camshare mounted to your Windows shared folder. You can then set this in a motion.cofig file as shown below:

target_dir /mnt/camshare

After this, motion will be saving all the videos in the shared folder of your Windows machine.

Fix Motion Autostart

You may experience a problem as the motion may not be started automatically once the Pi is rebooted. The reason is because the mounted folder on Windows is not ready when motion is trying to access it. To solve this, open the following file:

sudo nano /etc/init.d/motion

Then edit it by adding the following line to start a sequence:

sleep 30

Mounting the Camera

At this point, the surveillance camera can be mounted to destination point. You can now use any browser to access the live stream from the camera using the URL http://IPADDRESSOFRASPBERRY:8080. You can check for the port you are using on your system from the motion.conf file, then use it to replace the port 8080.
If you need to access the live stream from any location, then you will have to enable some dynamic domain services to the local network. With this, you will be able to connect to the local IP address from outside even after changes to the local

IP address. A good example of a service that can help you achieve this is dyn.com. After setting up the dynamic IP url, you will be in a position to access the camera stream from your browser despite your location. This also applies to you if you are using a mobile device.

There are multiple things you can do by use of the surveillance camera. You may make it send notifications once some motion has been detected. A temperature sensor can also be added. A battery pack can be added to the camera if there is a need for extra security. You should ensure that you buy one capable of charging while powering the Pi device at the same time.

Chapter 3- GPS Controlled Photo Taker

Whenever you are travelling, you will want to take pictures. However, some people hate to stop for this purpose. An automated photo take can help.

In this chapter, we will create an automated photo taker controlled by GPS. You will pre-select the places at which you need to take photos, and the app will automatically take them once you get near the place.

Requirements

- Raspberry Pi 3 Model B

- GPS Module U-blox NEO-6M with a 3m Active Antenna (STM32 51)

- PNY 7800 PowerPack

- GoPro HERO Series Camera

- GoPro 3-Way

You should hook a GPS module to the Raspberry Pi which will send a signal to GoPro through Wi-Fi. No soldering is needed; you just have to use a USB to plug the GPS module to your Raspberry Pi. You will use the Wi-Fi from the GoPro in the Raspberry Pi. The GoPro app can be used for configuring the SSD of the Wi-Fi. The Pi should be powered from a battery pack.

You should determine the coordinates for all the places at which you need to take photos. We will then write a Python script to help us calculate or determine the distance between the coordinates. Note that this script will start running immediately when the Raspberry Pi is turned on so as to check the coordinates.

You can use the GoPro API Library to establish a connection from the GoPro to the Raspberry Pi via Wi-Fi. The library can be installed by use of pip as shown below:

```
pip install goprocam
```

Note: in my case, I am in London, so I calculate the coordinates for the places I need to take photos in the city. I have written a Python script for this job. The script has an initialization of the camera as shown below:

```
camera = GoProCamera.GoPro()
```

The following line will then help us take the pictures:

```
camera.take_photo(0)
```

In this case, 0 refers to the time it will wait before taking the picture.

The gpsd-py3 should be installed. In my case, I have used pip. The following command will help you install this:

```
$ pip3 install gpsd-py3
```

The GPS daemon can then be pointed to GPS device. The line given below should be added to the "/etc/rc.local" file:

```
gpsd /dev/ttyACM0 -F /var/run/gpsd.sock
```

Our aim is to have our script executed once the Raspberry Pi is started. On the same file, that is, /etc/rc.local, add the following line:

```
python3 /home/pi/PictureScript.py
```

Note that "PictureScript.py" is the name of the script responsible for calculating the distance between the various London coordinates. Now that we have added it to the above file, it will be executed each time the Raspberry Pi is started.

PicturesScript.py

The calculations will done in this script. It will run on startup, then poll to check your coordinates against some list of coordinates you have select. The code for the script is as follows:

```python
import time
import gpsd
import math
from goprocam import GoProCamera
from goprocam import constants

#for calculating your current location
earthRadius = 6371

#Wait for Pi to boot then get the GoPro Wifi
time.sleep(20)

gpsd.connect()

camera = GoProCamera.GoPro()

#Saved Locations for the trip:
#Platform 9 3/4: 51.5322° , -0.1240°
#Abbey Road: 51.5321° , -0.1781°
#Buckingham 51.5014°, -0.1419°
#Big Ben 51.5007° , -0.1246°
#Tower of London 51.5081° , -0.0759°
#Tower Bridge 51.5055° , -0.0754°
#Shakespeare Globe 51.5081° , -0.0972°
#Sweetings 51.5125° , -0.0928°

#Create location arrays:
latitude = [51.5110, 51.5322, 51.5321, 51.5014, 51.5007, 51.5081, 51.5055,
51.5081, 51.5125]
longitude = [-0.1863, -0.1240, -0.1781, -0.1419, -0.1246, -0.0759, -0.0754, -
0.0972, -0.0928]

while True:
    received = False
    try:
       packet = gpsd.get_current()
        received = True
    except Exception:
        print("No signal")

    if received == True:
        #get my current position
        currentPost = packet.position()
        currentLat = currentPost[0]
        currentLon = currentPost[1]
        for location in range(len(latitude)):
            dLat = math.radians(latitude[location] - currentLat)
            dLon = math.radians(longitude[location] - currentLon)

            # a = sin²(Δφ/2) + cos φ1 · cos φ2 · sin²(Δλ/2)
            # c = 2 · atan2( √a, √(1-a) )
            #d = R · c
            a = math.sin(dLat/2) * math.sin(dLat/2) \
              + math.cos(math.radians(latitude[location])) \
              * math.cos(math.radians(currentLat)) * math.sin(dLon/2) \
              * math.sin(dLon/2)
            c = 2 * math.atan2(math.sqrt(a), math.sqrt(1-a))
            d = earthRadius * c

            if d < 0.01:
                camera.take_photo(0)

    time.sleep(1)
```

Note that we began by importing all the libraries needed with the use of the "import" keyword. A connection has then been established to the local gpsd in the line "gpsd.connect()". The line "camera = GoProCamera.GoPro()" helps us initialize the camera object. The locations have been stored in an array. The "while" loop helps us check the current coordinates we are at as well as the coordinates that have been saved.

We have used the haversine formula to calculate the distance between the coordinates. The variable "d" has been used to represent the distance between two coordinates. A picture will only be taken if d is found to be less than 10m, which is equivalent to 0.01km.

Chapter 4- Google Assistant in Raspberry Pi

In this project, we will be adding an indicator similar to that of Google Home for the Google Assistant running on the Raspberry Pi. The following components have been used in the project:

- Raspberry Pi 3 Model B

- Google AIY Projects Kit

- Microphone

- Speakers

- Adafruit NeoPixel Ring: WS2812 5050 RGB LED

- Jumper wires (generic)

- Everything ESP Wemos D1 Mini

- Arduino IDE

- Google Assistant SDK

After assembling all the above components, connect the Wemos D1 Mini and the Raspberry Pi as shown below:

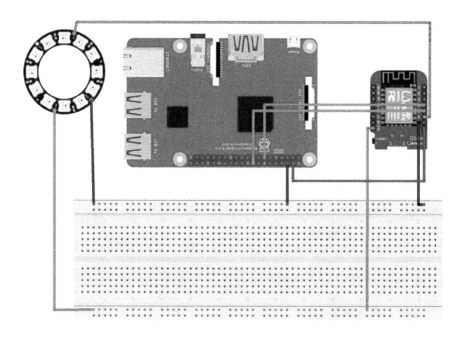

The pins can be changed depending on the board you are using and the neopixel ring. After that, upload the following code to your Arduino software:

```
#include <Adafruit_NeoPixel.h>

int numPixels = 12;
#define BUTTON_PIN1    D2
#define BUTTON_PIN2    D3
Adafruit_NeoPixel strip =
Adafruit_NeoPixel(numPixels, neoPixelPin, NEO_GRB +
NEO_KHZ800);

int start1 = 0;
int start2 = 3;
int start3 = 6;
int start4 = 9;
int brightness = 150;
```

```
int brightDirection = -15;
#define DELAY_TIME (50)
unsigned long startTime;

void setup() {
  pinMode(BUTTON_PIN1, INPUT);
  pinMode(BUTTON_PIN2, INPUT);
  strip.begin();
  strip.show();
  startTime = millis();
  activatecircle();
  activateblink();
}

void loop() {
  bool but1 = digitalRead(BUTTON_PIN1);
  bool but2 = digitalRead(BUTTON_PIN2);
  if (but1 == HIGH) {
    delay(10);
    if ( startTime + DELAY_TIME < millis() ) {
      activateblink();
      startTime = millis();
    }
  }
  else if (but2 == HIGH) {
    delay(10);
    if ( startTime + DELAY_TIME < millis() ) {
      activatecircle();
      startTime = millis();
    }
  }
  else {
    allOff();
  }
}
```

```
void allOff() {
  for ( int i = 0; i < numPixels; i++ ) {
    strip.setPixelColor(i, 0, 0, 0 );
  }
  strip.show();
}

void activatecircle() {
  adjustStarts();
  for ( int i = start1; i < start1 + 1; i++ ) {
    strip.setPixelColor(i, 23, 107, 239 );
  }
  for ( int i = start2; i < start2 + 1 ; i++ ) {
    strip.setPixelColor(i, 255, 62, 48 );
  }
  for ( int i = start3; i < start3 + 1; i++ ) {
    strip.setPixelColor(i, 247, 181, 41 );
  }
  for ( int i = start4; i < start4 + 1; i++ ) {
    strip.setPixelColor(i, 23, 156, 82 );
  }
  strip.show();
}

void activateblink() {
  for ( int i = start1; i < start1 + 1; i++ ) {
    strip.setPixelColor(i, 23, 107, 239 );
    strip.setBrightness(brightness);
    strip.show();
    adjustBrightness();
  }
  for ( int i = start2; i < start2 + 1 ; i++ ) {
    strip.setPixelColor(i, 255, 62, 48 );
    strip.setBrightness(brightness);
    strip.show();
    adjustBrightness();
```

```
  }
  for ( int i = start3; i < start3 + 1; i++ ) {
    strip.setPixelColor(i, 247, 181, 41 );
    strip.setBrightness(brightness);
    strip.show();
    adjustBrightness();
  }
  for ( int i = start4; i < start4 + 1; i++ ) {
    strip.setPixelColor(i, 23, 156, 82 );
    strip.setBrightness(brightness);
    strip.show();
   adjustBrightness();
  }
  strip.show();
}

void adjustStarts() {
  start1 = incrementStart(start1);
  start2 = incrementStart(start2);
  start3 = incrementStart(start3);
  start4 = incrementStart(start4);
}

int incrementStart(int startValue) {
  startValue = startValue + 1;
  if ( startValue == 12 )
    startValue = 0;
  return startValue;
}

void adjustBrightness() {
  brightness = brightness + brightDirection;
  if ( brightness < 0 ) {
    brightness = 0;
    brightDirection = -brightDirection;
  }
```

```
  else if ( brightness > 255 ) {
    brightness = 255;
    brightDirection = -brightDirection;
  }

  Serial.println( brightness );
}
```

Note that you can change the pin numbers depending on the board you are using. We have also defined 4 pixels, each representing a Google color. The "for" loop helps us set different colors for the pixels in intervals of 20.

Chapter 5- Raspberry Pi 3 Gaming

To be able to stream Steam to your Raspberry Pi, you should have the following components:

- Raspberry Pi 3

- Steam installed with steam games

- 5V 2.5A Power Supply

- Xbox 360 Wired Controller

- 8GB+ Micro SD card

- A Windows PC with GTX650+ NVidia Graphics Card

A 2.5A power supply should be used to power the Raspberry Pi. Samsung SD Cards are the best, as they support the Wire Laveling technology which makes the card serve for a longer time. Your computer should be installed with Windows 7, 8, 8.1 or 10.

Ensure that your Raspberry Pi 3 is installed with the latest version of Raspbian OS.

Next, install Moonlight into the Raspberry Pi 3. The Raspbian command line will be needed for this task.

Let us add the source from which we will download Moonlight by running the following command:

```
sudo bash -c 'printf "deb
http://archive.itimmer.nl/raspbian/moonlight jessie
main\n" >> /etc/apt/sources.list'
```

We can then update the system and install the Moonlight by running the following two commands:

```
sudo apt-get update
```

```
sudo apt-get install moonlight-embedded
```

You will then have Moonlight installed in your Raspberry Pi.

Discovering the Computer's IP Address

You should discover the IP address of the machine having the Steam installed on it. To do this, press the Windows key on your computer, begin to type CMD, then hit the enter key. A command prompt will be started, so type the following command on it:

```
ipconfig
```

You will then be able to determine the IP address of your computer. Once you have obtained it, you can go back to setting up Moonlight.

Configuring Moonlight

It is time to pair the Raspberry Pi with Gamestream service in the GeForce Experience. You just have to run the following command in the command prompt of the Pi, with the 192.168... being the IP address of your computer:

```
moonlight pair 192.168…
```

Note the PIN number generated by the Raspberry Pi, then go back to your computer installed with Steam.
The GeForce should now pop up some window which will prompt the PIN to be entered. Type the PIN, then click CONNECT. You should now see your Raspberry Pi display "paired".

Starting Moonlight

Now that you have paired up everything, you should connect the Xbox 360 controller, then run the following command on the Raspberry Pi 3's command prompt to start Moonlight:

```
moonlight stream -1080 -30fps -app Steam
```

It is possible for you to change a number of settings such as the -720 instead of -1080, and -60fps instead of the -30fps if you need to increase the frames. You will then be done!

Chapter 6- Creating a Node.JS Web Server

In this chapter, we will be building a Node.js server on the Raspberry Pi 3. You will also familiarize yourself with resin.io basics. You will know how to get the Raspberry Pi 3 online and then upload some Node.js code to it.

Begin by assembling the following components:

- A Raspberry Pi 3 Model B
- A 4GB or a larger microSD card
- An ethernet cable (optional)
- A micro USB cable
- A 2A USB micro power supply (optional)
- A resin.io account

If you have not created a resin.io account, just open its home page and begin to sign up. You will be asked to set up some SSH key so that you can push the code securely.

SSH keys use the concept of public key cryptography so that the connection can be secured when you are sending your code. For your Git connection to remain secured, you should add a public SSH key.

Enter your SSH Key

We need your public SSH key to authenticate you when you push changes to your application's git repo. Don't know what this is? Check out GitHub's instructions.

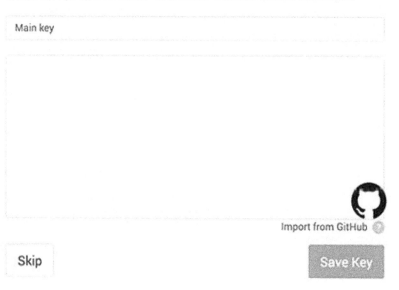

Main key

Import from GitHub

Skip

Save Key

Paste the public key into the provided box, then click "Save Key". If you need to import the key from Github, just click the Octocat icon.

Creating the Application

To create the application, type the name for the application, choose the Raspberry Pi 3 from the drop down, then click on the create button. You will be taken to the dashboard for your app.

Adding the First Device

All the devices that have been connected to your application should be shown on the dashboard, together with their logs and statuses.

Click on "Download resinOS" to begin downloading the resin.io operating system image for the application. A drop down will be shown with a list of all available versions. Choose the latest.

A prompt will appear asking you to specify the means of connecting the device to the Internet. You can use either an Ethernet cable or Wi-Fi. For the former, you don't need to do any configuration; but for the latter, you will have to configure the network SSID and the passphrase.

Once you have chosen the connectivity option, click on "Download Device OS" and the resion.io OS will be downloaded together with the necessary settings for the network and the application. After the download is complete, you will get a file with an .img extension, which is the image.

Creating a Bootable SD Card

It is now time to send the .img file to the SD card. Etcher is the best tool for this purpose, as it will help you write the image to the SD card and validate it. Install it now!

You can also use other SD card writers such as win32diskimager.

Once the Etcher has been installed, just start it. The following steps will help you create a bootable SD card with the resinOS:

1. Click on "Select image" button, then find the resinOS `.img` file for your applications.
2. If you have not already done this, insert the SD card into the computer. Etcher will detect it automatically. If you have inserted more than one SD card, you will have to select the right one.
3. Click on "Flash!" button.

The Etcher will create a bootable SD card for you and perform a validation as to whether it was done correctly. Once the process is complete, the SD card will be ejected.

Device Setup

Insert the SD card into your Raspberry Pi 3, then establish a connection to the Internet. Insert the Micro USB cable to power the Raspberry Pi 3.

It will take about 3 minutes to see the Raspberry Pi 3 on the resin.io dashboard. As you wait for the partitions on the SD card to be expanded, install a custom Linux environment, then establish a secure connection with the servers.

Deploying the Code

Since we have connected one or two devices to the resin.io application, we can go ahead and deploy some code and then begin to build something.

You can begin by creating an Express.js web server to serve a static page on the port :80. Here is the code for the server.js:

```
var express = require('express');
var app = express();

// reply to request with "Hello World!"
app.get('/', function (req, res) {
  res.send('Hello World!');
});

//start a server on port 80 and log its start to our
console
var server = app.listen(80, function () {
  var port = server.address().port;
  console.log('Example app listening on port ', port);
});
```

Since the project can be accessed on Github, we can clone it by running the following command:

```
$ git clone https://github.com/resin-io-
projects/simple-server-node.git
```

After the repository has been cloned, you can change your directory to the one newly created, the simple-server-node directory, then run the following command to add resin git remote endpoint:

```
$ cd simple-server-node
$ git remote add resin
<USERNAME>@git.resin.io:<USERNAME>/<APPNAME>.git
```

We will have set a reference in the local Git repository to the resin.io application remote repository. After pushing to the remote repository, it will be compiled, then be built on the servers, then deployed to each device in our application fleet. The following command will help deploy the code to all devices contained in the application:

```
$ git push resin master
```

To replace the source code of your application with some new source tree, you can run the "`git push resin master -force`" command so as to force the push.

If you see the friendly unicorn mascot in the terminal, know that the compilation was successful. This code should now be stored in the image registry.

All devices connected to the application fleet will download and execute the application.

At this point, you should have a Node.js web server running on the device and see logs on the dashboard. If you open the "Actions" page for the device, enable the public URL and it will be accessible from any place in the world. If you follow the URL, you will get a page with "Hello, World!" text. You can also point the browser to the IP address of your machine.

The root directory of our project will have a number of files including Dockerfile.template, package.json and server.js. The .template file will allow you to define the variables for the template like "%%RESIN_MACHINE_NAME%%" which will help you to push a repository to multiple and different architecture fleets.

Below is the first line of the Dockerfile.template file:

```
FROM resin/%%RESIN_MACHINE_NAME%%-node:slim
```

The placeholder "%%RESIN_MACHINE_NAME%%" will be replaced with the name of the resin device. Since you are using a Raspberry Pi 3, this line will be as follows:

FROM `resin/raspberrypi3-node:slim`

This tells the resin builder that we need to use this image as the base. There is a ":slim" tag associated with the base image denoting what the stripped-down version to have minimal packages needs to run the node, meaning that there will be no node-gyp as well as other build essentials.
The following lines have been commented out:

```
RUN apt-get update && apt-get install -yq \
  alsa-utils libasound2-dev && \
  apt-get clean && rm -rf /var/lib/apt/lists/*
```

This demonstrates how the apt-get can be used for installation of dependencies in a container. We will be installing some useful Linux sound utilities. The whole code for the .template file should be as follows:

```
FROM resin/%%RESIN_MACHINE_NAME%%-node:slim

WORKDIR /usr/src/app

COPY package.json package.json

RUN JOBS=MAX npm install --production --unsafe-perm &&
npm cache clean && rm -rf /tmp/*
```

COPY ../

ENV INITSYSTEM on

CMD ["npm", "start"]

The WORDIR helps us set the working directory for COPY, RUN and CMD commands which follow it.

We can now go ahead and build the node.js dependencies and modules using the RUN command. We have also used the – production flag to build and clear the cache to keep our final image smaller.

After the npm install, the rest of the code will be copied to the working directory, and this is done later so that the builds can benefit from the build caching. A full npm install will only be triggered once something in the package.json file is changed.

Below is the code for package.json file:

```
{
  "name": "simple-server-node",
  "version": "1.0.0",
  "description": "A simple Expressjs Web server on
resin.io",
  "main": "server.js",
  "scripts": {
    "test": "echo \"Error: no test specified\" && exit 1",
    "start": "node server.js"
  },
  "repository": {
    "type": "git",
    "url": "git+https://github.com/resin-io-
projects/simple-server-node.git"
```

```
  },
  "keywords": [
    "resin.io",
    "webserver",
    "nodejs",
    "expressjs"
  ],
  "author": "Stefan <stefan@resin.io>",
  "license": "Apache-2.0",
  "bugs": {
    "url": "https://github.com/resin-io-projects/simple-
server-node/issues"
  },
  "homepage": "https://github.com/resin-io-projects/simple-
server-node#readme",
  "dependencies": {
    "express": "*"
  }
}
```

In the section for dependencies, we have defined the node modules and the versions we need to use in the application. The scripts allow us point to the server.js as the starting point for whole application.

Web Terminal

This is built on the dashboard and helps in running commands and checking log files. To start it on your device, the following are expected:

1. An online device
2. A running container

Number 1 is easy, but number 2 is somehow hard. If the

docker's main process crashes or ends, the container will stop and your web terminal will have nothing to which to SSH. To ensure that the container is always up and running during development, use the system init system.

To launch a session, navigate to >_Terminal page for your device then hit the button for "Start the terminal session". Some seconds will elapse before a new session can be established and you will be ready to go.

Resin Sync for Faster Development

At this point, you are aware how to provision a device, then push code. The resin sync command line tool will allow you to sync your source code quickly, then file the changes across the devices in the fleet.

Setting up the Resin Sync

The Resin sync comes with the resin CLI. It will allow you to do all the tasks from the command line.

For you to install the resin CLI and sync, your machine should be installed with node.js 4.0.0 and above. The following command will help you install resin:

```
$ npm install --global --production resin-cli
```

You must have administrative privileges to be able to run the above command. Once the CLI has been installed, use your resin account to login:

```
$ resin login
```

You will be prompted to choose the best login method, with the best being web authorization. This method will present a dialog in your browser, and you will be asked to authorize the use of the CLI.

Set Up Node.js Cross-Compilation

There is no need for cross-compilation when using resin sync and the Node.js because it's an interpreted language. Begin by launching the terminal in our previous directory to begin using the resin sync.
Make some trivial change to the source code, then run the following command:

```
$ resin sync --source . --destination /usr/src/app
```

You will be prompted to choose a device, and all the files in the root of the directory will be synced to /usr/src/app on the chosen device and the container will be restarted. You will get an output related to the one given below:

```
resin:simple-server-node shaun$ resin sync --source .
--destination /usr/src/app
```

```
Getting information for device:
5dc2c87ea2caf79bc4e25ae638c6d5a35a75cecf22e8f914331dc
b2f588f4b
Application container stopped.
Synced /usr/src/app on 5dc2c87.
Application container started.

resin sync completed successfully!
```

After about 30 seconds, the new code will be up and running. The resin SSH is one of the most useful features of the resin-cli. It will allow you to perform a quick SSH into the container which is running the device, then pull out logs or run some test commands.

With the device online and having logged into the CLI, you are able to access the container by use of "resin ssh <uuid>". The following example demonstrates this:

```
resin:simple-server-node nicohsam$ resin ssh 5dc2c87
Connecting with: 5dc2c87
root@raspberrypi3-5dc2c8:/# uname -a
Linux Raspberry Pi 3-5dc2c8 3.10.93 #1 SMP PREEMPT
Wed June 14 11:25:12 CEST 2017 armv7l GNU/Linux
```

The resin.io also has many other features of which you can take advantage.

Chapter 7- Building a Smart TV

In this chapter, we will show you how to build a Smart TV with Raspberry Pi 3, Node.JS and Socket.io. Begin by assembling the following components:

- The Raspberry Pi 33 Model B
- A USB WiFi dongle or an Ethernet cable
- 8 GB+SD/MicroSD card
- Raspbian, that is, a fork of Debian developed for Raspberry Pi
- Node.js:
    - Socket.io for handling the connection between the remote and the TV via websockets
    - Express for handling basic http requests
    - Omxcontrol for some simple module for controlling the OMXPlayer
- OMXPlayer
- Youtube-dl, which is a script to allow us download YouTube videos
- Chromium Browser
- Quo.js for handling swipe gestures on mobile web app
- YouTube API
- HTML5, JavaScript, CSS3 transitions, and Moustache in the form of a template engine

The first step should be to install the Raspbian and the Node. js in your Raspberry Pi. My assumption is that you are aware of how to install them, so we will not discuss it.

Installation of Chromium and YouTube-dl

You can use apt-get or build the chromium browser from the source. Use the following command:

```
sudo apt-get install chromium-browser
```

If you need to have a better display, install the MC core fonts by running the following command:

```
sudo apt-get install ttf-mscorefonts-installer
```

You can then run the following commands to install and then update the Youtube-dl script:

```
sudo apt-get install youtube-dl
```

```
sudo youtube-dl -U
```

The Chromium is not hardware accelerated, and it will be a bad idea for us to stream idea to the browser. The Youtube-dl is the best alternative; the video will be downloaded and streamed in the OMX-player, this being hardware accelerated in the Pi.

Note that the OMX-player comes installed in the Raspian OS.

Basic Shellcode

If you need to establish a connection to the Raspberry Pi via SSH, you should first update the DISPLAY environment variables by use of the following command:

```
export DISPLAY=:0.0
```

The graphical output you get from the session will point to the first display which has been connected to Raspberry Pi. The following command will help you check all available environment variables:

```
env
```

You can now test the Chromium while in the Kiosk mode:

```
chromium --kiosk http://www.google.com
```

The Youtube-dl can be tested as follows:

```
youtube-dl youtube_video_url
```

You can modify the Youtube-dl command by adding the following options:

```
youtube-dl  -o "%(id)s.%(ext)s" -f /22/18
youtube_video_url
```

Once you have downloaded the video, you can attempt to play it by use of the OMX-Player as shown below:

```
omxplayer youtube_video_file
```

Server-Side Scripting

The project file hierarchy should be as follows:

- public

    - js
    - css
    - images
    - fonts
    - index.html
    - remote.html

- app.js
- package.json

The file Package.json will be needed by the npm for auto-installation of dependencies and storage of the other metadata about the project. This should be as follows:

```
{
    "name": "RasPi.TV",
    "version": "0.0.1",
    "private": false,
    "scripts": {
        "start": "node app.js"
    },
    "dependencies": {
    "express": "3.1.1",
    "socket.io":"0.9.14",
```

```
    "omxcontrol":"*"
    }
}
```

You can install the dependencies by running the following command on the terminal:

```
npm install
```

A node with the name "node-modules" will be created in the project directory. If you would like to use git, create a .gitignore file and add the line "node_modules" to the file, which will help you ignore the node_modules folder from being added to the git project.

Create the file app.js then begin to create the basic HTTP server with the Express.js:

```
var express = require('express')
  , app = express()
  , server = require('http').createServer(app)
  , path = require('path')

// all environments
app.set('port', process.env.TEST_PORT || 8080);
app.use(express.favicon());
app.use(express.logger('dev'));
app.use(express.bodyParser());
app.use(express.methodOverride());
app.use(express.static(path.join(__dirname,
'public')));

//Routes
app.get('/', function (req, res) {
```

```
  res.sendfile(__dirname + '/public/index.html');
});

app.get('/remote', function (req, res) {
  res.sendfile(__dirname + '/public/remote.html');
});

server.listen(app.get('port'), function(){
  console.log('Express server listening on port ' +
app.get('port'));
});
```

Above is the basic configuration of the Express HTTP server. For you to be able to test it, you should first create the static files, the remote.html and the index.html in the public directory. Write the "Hello, World" message into these pages and then execute them from the terminal:

```
node app.js
```

Or use:

```
npm start
```

For this to work, you must have added the following code snippet to the file Package.json:

```
...
"scripts": {
        "start": "node app.js"
    },
...
```

On the stdout of the server init, you will get the following:

```
Express server listening on port 8080
```

If you need to test the static pages, run your app in the background by use of & as shown below:

```
node app.js &
```

Our Node.js web server is now capable of serving the static files. We can launch our Chromium in the Kiosk mode, then test the web pages:

```
chromium --kiosk http://localhost:8080
```

Integrating Socket.io

For the purpose of providing real time connectivity on each browser, the Socket.io will choose the most capable transport during runtime, and the API will not be affected.

To integrate the Socket.io, you only have to add the code given below to the app.js file:

```
var express = require('express')
  , app = express()
  , server = require('http').createServer(app)
  , path = require('path')
  , io = require('socket.io').listen(server)
  , spawn = require('child_process').spawn
```

The logs can be minified by adding the following:

```
//Socket.io Config
io.set('log level', 1);
```

When using Socket.io for development, just know that you are developing a chat-like application.

The Socket.io server is now ready; but for now, it can do nothing. Let us implement the code that will process the messages and events sent from client to server.

The integration of Socket.io on the server side is as follows:

```
io.sockets.on('connection', function (socket) {
    socket.emit('message', { message: 'welcome to the
chat' });
    socket.on('send', function (data) {
        //Emit to all
        io.sockets.emit('message', data);
    });
});
```

The server should be emitting the message "message" after a connection to a new client. It will also wait for the event "send" so as to process data and emit it to all the clients that have been connected.

There are two types of clients in our case, that is, the rPi display (TV) and mobile web app (remote).

```
var ss;
//Socket.io Server
io.sockets.on('connection', function (socket) {
```

```
socket.on("screen", function(data){
  socket.type = "screen";
  //Save the screen socket
  ss = socket;
  console.log("Screen ready...");
});

socket.on("remote", function(data){
  socket.type = "remote";
  console.log("Remote ready...");
  if(ss != undefined){
      console.log("Synced...");
  }
});
)};
```

Implementing Client-Side Web Socket

Add the script given below to the file remote.html:

```
<script src="/socket.io/socket.io.js"> </script>
 <script>
   //use http://raspberryPi.local if your using Avahi Service
      //or use your RasperryPi IP instead
      var socket = io.connect('http://raspberrypi.local:8080');
    socket.on('connect', function(data){
      socket.emit('screen');
    });
  </script>
```

The following script should then be added to index.html:

```
<script src="/socket.io/socket.io.js"> </script>
<script>
   //use http://raspberryPi.local if your using Avahi Service
      //or use your RasperryPi IP instead
      var socket = io.connect('http://raspberrypi.local:8080');
    socket.on('connect', function(data){
      socket.emit('screen');
```

```
    });
</script>
```

With Node.js, we are able to run system commands in the given privileges of the child process. You can also pass arguments to commands, and performing piping of output from commands.

The Node.js commands can be executed as follows from the Child process:

```
spawn('echo',['foobar']);
```

If you are in need of piping the response to some other call, the callback function given below should be provided to the function:

```
//Run then pipe the shell script output
function run_shell(cmd, args, cb, end) {
    var spawn = require('child_process').spawn,
        child = spawn(cmd, args),
        me = this;
    child.stdout.on('data', function (buffer) { cb(me, buffer) });
    child.stdout.on('end', end);
}
```

Adding OMXControl

With the OMXControl module, you are able to control the OMX-Player via HTTP. The following will be needed in the main file for the project:

```
var omx = require('omxcontrol');
```

```
//use it with express
app.use(omx());
```

The OMXControl module will create the routes given below for the purpose of controlling the video playback:

```
http://localhost:8080/omx/start/:filename
http://localhost:8080/omx/pause
http://localhost:8080/omx/quit
```

The complete app.js file should be as follows:

```
var express = require('express')
  , app = express()
  , server = require('http').createServer(app)
  , path = require('path')
  , io = require('socket.io').listen(server)
  , spawn = require('child_process').spawn
  , omx = require('omxcontrol');

app.set('port', process.env.TEST_PORT || 8080);
app.use(express.favicon());
app.use(express.logger('dev'));
app.use(express.bodyParser());
app.use(express.methodOverride());
app.use(express.static(path.join(__dirname, 'public')));
app.use(omx());

app.get('/', function (req, res) {
  res.sendfile(__dirname + '/public/index.html');
});

app.get('/remote', function (req, res) {
  res.sendfile(__dirname + '/public/remote.html');
});

io.set('log level', 1);

server.listen(app.get('port'), function(){
  console.log('Express server listening on port ' + app.get('port'));
});

function run_shell(cmd, args, cb, end) {
    var spawn = require('child_process').spawn,
```

```
            child = spawn(cmd, args),
            me = this;
    child.stdout.on('data', function (buffer) { cb(me, buffer) });
    child.stdout.on('end', end);
}


var ss;
io.sockets.on('connection', function (socket) {

 socket.on("screen", function(data){
   socket.type = "screen";
   ss = socket;
   console.log("Screen ready...");
 });
 socket.on("remote", function(data){
   socket.type = "remote";
   console.log("Remote ready...");
 });

 socket.on("controll", function(data){
    console.log(data);
   if(socket.type === "remote"){

     if(data.action === "tap"){
         if(ss != undefined){
            ss.emit("controlling", {action:"enter"});
            }
        }
      else if(data.action === "swipeLeft"){
       if(ss != undefined){
          ss.emit("controlling", {action:"goLeft"});
          }
       }
      else if(data.action === "swipeRight"){
        if(ss != undefined){
          ss.emit("controlling", {action:"goRight"});
            }
       }
    }
  }
 });


 socket.on("video", function(data){

    if( data.action === "play"){
    var id = data.video_id,
         url = "http://www.youtube.com/watch?v="+id;

    var runShell = new run_shell('youtube-dl',['-o','%(id)s.%(ext)s','-
f','/18/22',url],
        function (me, buffer) {
            me.stdout += buffer.toString();
```

159

```
        socket.emit("loading",{output: me.stdout});
        console.log(me.stdout)
    },
    function () {
        //child = spawn('omxplayer',[id+'.mp4']);
        omx.start(id+'.mp4');
    });
}

});
});
```

Client Side Scripting

We can now begin to script on the client side.

Dashboard and Remote Mobile-app

We will not discuss how to create the front-end of the app. Instead of having to create a remote made up of buttons, we can choose to use the Quo.js. This is a nice cross-platform swipe gestures library for JavaScript.

```
$$(".r-container").swipeLeft(function(){
socket.emit('control',{action:"swipeLeft"});
});
```

For me to send the "Control" message back to the server with "swipeLeft" as the data action, I can use the approach given below. The server will send the message to the screen, and the screen client will selected square to next app.

The following should be added to the between the <head></head> tags in the HTML:

```
<link rel="apple-touch-icon" href="images/custom_icon.png"/>
```

```html
<link rel="apple-touch-startup-image" href="images/startup.png">
<meta name="viewport" content="width=device-width initial-scale=1, maximum-scale=1, user-scalable=no" />
<meta name="apple-mobile-web-app-title" content="Remote">
<meta name="apple-mobile-web-app-capable" content="yes">
```

Chapter 8- Installing Kodi on Raspberry Pi 3

The easiest way to have cheap XBMC, HD streamer is by installing Kodi on your Raspberry Pi 3. Kodi is one of the best of the streaming software that can help you create a speedy and dedicated media dongle. You should have the Raspberry Pi 3, Linux distribution and a few cables. Assemble the components, then follow the steps given below:

Installing Kodi

To use the Raspberry Pi as a media center, use any of the available purpose-built OSes and these will help you get started. I prefer using OSMC, which is a version of Kodi readily optimized to be used in the Pi device.

If you are not familiar with microSD card flashing, Linux distros and disk images, it is advisable that you use the Raspbmc, a default OS option that comes with NOOBS installer for Raspberry Pi Foundation. To use this, follow the normal guidelines for setting up the Raspberry Pi, then choose Raspbmc as the distro package to install other than the Raspbian.

Wi-Fi Setup

After installation and boot up, you should setup the Wi-Fi.

Open the Programs tab, then the Raspbmc settings menu. You will be allowed to enter the details for your Wi-Fi network such as the name and password. After, you will be connected to the Wi-Fi.

Adding the Remote Control

At this point, we should add a remote control to the Raspberry Pi. You don't need to control it with a keyboard and mouse as this is tiresome. If your TV is capable of supporting HDMI CEC,you are lucky as the standard TV remote will be compatible with the Pi. You will then be able to browse the content while seated on your coach.

It is also possible for you to control this via a web interface. You only have to go to the Raspbmc's system info menu, note down the IP address of the Raspberry Pi, then type the address into the browser. However, since you are using it from the browser, you will have to use the http:// prefix and the two computers should be on the same network. After the web UI has been opened, choose the "remote" tab, and a control interface will be provided that you can use to navigate to the contents.

For smartphone and tablet users, it is also possible for you to control the Pi from the device.

Playing the Files

Now that everything has been setup, we can go to the most

important part, which is watching TV and movies. This is straight forward. Just plug in the flash drive or an external hard drive having the media in it. The Raspberry Pi will detect this automatically.

You can open the necessary tab, whether music, movies or video, then choose your storage device. You will see the files ready for playing. If you have a NAS drive, the Raspbmc is able to read and play the files from there, but the use of a thumb drive is the simplest way of doing it.

Setting up AirPlay

If you are a fan of Apple with a lot of content from iTunes, it is also possible for you to setup the Raspberry Pi as an AirPlay receiver. Open the AirPlay tab from the services tab, then tick the "allow XBMC to receive AirPlay content" option. Once you are done, the Apple device will detect the Raspberry Pi as an AirPlay Receiver, and you will be in a position to see all the contents from the iTunes store.

After doing all the above, you can start to stream your content in HD. It will be a nice experience as the Raspbmc is updated on a constant basis, and it provides a number of add-ons and options that can be altered to give you the kind of experience you need.

Chapter 9- Face Detection in Raspberry Pi

In this project, we will use the OpenCV to detect faces in the Raspberry Pi 3. To detect objects by use of cascade files, you should first get the cascade files.

The following components are needed for this project:

- Raspberry Pi 3 Model B

- Raspberry Pi Camera Module

You should also already have your Pi installed with Raspbian OS. You need to have installed PuTTY, an open source software for telnet and SSH client. We will be using the PuTTY software to access our Raspberry Pi remotely.

Your machine should also be installed with Open Source Computer Vision Library (OpenCV). This computer vision software can be used for machine learning. The software was developed to help provide a common infrastructure for the computer vision applications and for acceleration of the use of machine learning perception in commercial products. The OpenCV can easily be used in business, and it is easy for to customize the code. The library has over 2500 optimized algorithms that can be used for recognition of faces, identification of objects, tracking camera movements, classifying human actions in videos and extracting D models for objects.

You should first install the OpenCV into your computer. The

steps for doing this have already being discussed in previous chapters, so consult them.

Enabling the Camera

For the purpose of face recognition, you have to configure and enable the camera. To enable the camera, run the following command:

```
Sudo raspi-config
```

A small window will pop up with a number of options from which you can choose the one you want. Choose the option that says "Enable/Disable connection to the Raspberry Pi Camera". The password for the default user needs to be changed, so ensure you have done this for your camera. Set the interfacing options for the camera module. Lastly, you will be asked whether you need the camera module to be enabled, so choose "Yes". You will get a notification that your camera module has been enabled.

To test if this was successful, you just have to take a picture to know whether it is working correctly.

Chapter 10- Raspberry Pi Print Server

In this chapter, we will help you learn how to setup a print server in the Raspberry Pi. Installation of the software is somewhat easy, but much work is needed to configure it and make the Windows network find the print server. After that, you will have your printer setup, and this can be moved to any location and be accessible to multiple computers.

This will be done by use of software named CUPS (Common Unix Printing System). It forms the backbone of most printing software in Linux. It is the one responsible for communicating with the printer and getting printing work done. The following components are needed for this chapter:

- Raspberry Pi 3
- Micro SD Card
- Ethernet Cord or Wi-Fi dongle (Pi 3 has its Wi-Fi inbuilt)
- USB Printer

Optional:

- Raspberry Pi Case
- USB Keyboard
- USB Mouse

<u>**Installing the Print Server Software**</u>

The software is available through Debian Jessie packages. First, update the Pi to ensure you are using the latest version of the software. Run the following commands on the terminal:

```
sudo apt-get update
sudo apt-get upgrade
```

After the Pi has been updated, we can begin to install the print software. This will be CUPS that can manage printers attached through a USB or via the network. Run the following command on the terminal:

```
sudo apt-get install cups
```

After the installation of the software is complete, you will be required to perform a number of configurations. The Pi user should be added to lpadmin group. With this, the Pi user will be in a position to access the administrative functions for CUPS with no need for the super user. The user can be added to the group by running the following command:

```
sudo usermod -a -G lpadmin pi
```

For CUPS to be accessible throughout the network, we have to configure this. With the current setting, any non-localhost traffic will be blocked. To make it accept all traffic, we must run the following command:

```
sudo cupsctl --remote-any
sudo /etc/init.d/cups restart
```

At this point, we should be able to access the print server from any computer located on the network. If you don't know the IP address of your Pi, then run the following command:

```
hostname -I
```

Once you are aware of the IP address, use it on the browser as shown below:

```
http://192.168.1.105:631
```

SAMBA also needs to be setup correctly so that Windows can identify the print server correctly. The next section helps you set this up.

Set up SAMBA

For you to be in a position to use the print server with Windows in the correct way, you will have to set up SAMBA. We will install and configure it so that it can use the CUPS print drivers correctly.
Run the following command on the terminal:

```
sudo apt-get install samba
```

The command will help you install SAMBA. Let's open its file to make the necessary configuration changes:

```
sudo nano /etc/samba/smb.conf
```

Press Ctrl + V to move to the bottom of the file. Now that you are at the bottom of the file, you can add the following section; but if it is there, you will only have to change it to match the following;

```
# CUPS printing.
[printers]
comment = All Printers
browseable = no
path = /var/spool/samba
printable = yes
guest ok = yes
read only = yes
create mask = 0700

# Windows clients will look for this share name as a
source of the downloadable
# printer drivers
[print$]
comment = Printer Drivers
path = /var/lib/samba/printers
browseable = yes
read only = no
guest ok = no
```

Hit Ctrl + to save the file so as to exit. We can then restart SAMBA for the changes to take effect. The following command will help us do this:

```
sudo /etc/init.d/samba restart
```

Add the Printer to CUPS

This can be done easily, but we should first load the web

interface for CUPS. If you are not sure of the IP address for the Pi, run the following command on the terminal;

```
hostname -I
```

Now that you are aware of the IP address of your Pi, open the browser, then type the following address:

```
https://192.168.1.105:631
```

Make sure you replace the above IP address with the one for your Pi. In the web interface opened, click on "Administration". Once the Administration window is open, click on "Add Printer".

A new window will pop up from which you will be able to choose the printer you need. Choose that printer, then click on "Continue". Your printer may not show up on the screen. To solve this, ensure that your printer is connected to one of the Pi's ports and that it is turned on. It will show automatically. If the problem persists, restart the Pi.

You can then choose the model for your printer. CUPS is capable of detecting this automatically and choosing the right driver. However, if this fails to work, you will have to browse through the list, then choose the right driver. Once everything is setup correctly, click the "Add Printer" button.

Next, set the name and description you need. You can also set the location in case you have multiple printers and need to work with them.

The option "Share This Printer" should be enabled to ensure that the other computers in the network can access the printer. Once done, click "Continue". You will be presented with a new screen that will allow you to change some aspects of the printer. These include the print quality, the page's print size as well as other options. After this, we will add the newly set print server to Windows.

Adding the Print Server to Windows

For you to add the CUPS printer to Windows, a lot of work may have to be done as you will be expected to choose the necessary drivers for the connection to be successful.

To start, open the Windows network page by loading up "This PC" or "My Computer". You will then click on "network" from the sidebar.

Double click on your Pi and you will be asked for the username and password. Press enter, and if it fails to work, type in pi as the username. A window showing you all the printers available in your Pi will be presented. Identify the printer you need to connect to and double click it. You may see a warning message, but simply click "OK" to continue.

A connection with the printer will then be loaded up. If you need to make it the default printer for your computer, click on Printer, then "Set as Default Printer". The printer will be made available for use by any program and it will have been added to the computer successfully. You can then test the printer by trying to print a file.

You may experience some problems when trying to print. In such a case, it will be good for you to ensure that you have selected the right printer driver in both Windows and CUPS.

You also need to ensure that your printer is on. Some printers will not turn on automatically once a file has been sent to it for printing. You can then enjoy printing. Congratulations!

Chapter 11- Setting up a Weather Station

In this chapter, we will show you how to use Sense HAT and Raspberry Pi 3 to set up a weather station. You will then be able to use this station to monitor the weather from your room or from anywhere.

The Sense HAT is equipment with numerous sensors contained in a single package. It provides you with an easy-to-add sensor to your Pi without extra circuitry. It has three primary sensors, and we will use them to detect humidity, temperature and pressure. The code is written in Python.

Begin by assembling the following components:

- Raspberry Pi 3

- Sense HAT

- Micro SD Card

- Raspberry Pi Case (optional)

Before beginning, first place the Sense HAT in the correct GPIO pins. Then update the Pi to ensure it is running the latest software version:

```
sudo apt-get update
sudo apt-get upgrade
```

We can then install the Sense Hat software package which will provide us with all libraries necessary to interact with the Sense HAT. After installation, a reboot will be necessary for the new software to begin working effectively:

```
sudo apt-get install sense-hat
sudo reboot
```

Let us create the file for the script by running the following command;

```
sudo nano ~/sensehat_test.py
```

Add the following line to the file:

```
from sense_hat import SenseHat
```

The purpose of the above line is to import the Sense Hat module from the sense_hat library. Add the following line:

```
sense = SenseHat()
```

The above line will help establish a link to the Sense Hat library and initialize it for us to begin making calls to it. Add the next line given below to the script:

```
sense.show_message("Hello World")
```

The above line should write the message, "Hello World", so you should see the message scroll across RGB lights.

Press Ctrl + X, then hit Y plus enter to exit the file. You will have saved the file, so run it by executing the following command from the terminal:

```
sudo python ~/sensehat_test.py
```

You should see the "Hello World" message scrolling.

We can now begin to write the script for the weather station. Create the script file by running the following command on the terminal:

```
sudo nano ~/weather_script.py
```

Add the following lines to the script:

```
#!/usr/bin/python
from sense_hat import SenseHat
import time
import sys
```

The above lines help us import the libraries needed. Add the following code to the script, so that you end up with the following in your file:

```
#!/usr/bin/python
from sense_hat import SenseHat
import time
import sys

sense = SenseHat()
sense.clear()

try:
        while True:
```

```
            temp = sense.get_temperature()
            temp = round(temp, 1)
            print("Temperature C",temp)

            humidity = sense.get_humidity()
            humidity = round(humidity, 1)
            print("Humidity :",humidity)

            pressure = sense.get_pressure()
            pressure = round(pressure, 1)
            print("Pressure:",pressure)

            time.sleep(1)
except KeyboardInterrupt:
        pass
```

A link to the sense hat library has been created, The LED matrix has been cleared, so you will see all the LEDs go off. The indentation for the "while" should be maintained. The line:

```
temp = sense.get_temperature()
```

helps us retrieve the temperature by calling the sensor. The output will be in Celsius. If you need to convert it to Fahrenheit, use the following line:

```
temp = 1.8 * round(temp, 1)  + 32
```

The pressure and humidity sensors have been read in the same way to that of temperature.

Save and exit the code by pressing Ctrl + X, then Y, and hit enter. Run the script by typing the following command on the terminal:

```
sudo python ~/weather_script.py
```

The values for temperature, humidity and pressure will be shown. To stop your script from running, just hit ctrl + c.

Using LED Matrix

We now need to perform an improvement to our weather station. We will change it so that the results can be displayed on the LED matrix. Open the script by running the following command:

```
sudo nano ~/weather_script.py
```

Add the line given below just above the "time.sleep(1);" line:

```
sense.show_message("Temperature C" + str(temp) + "Humidity:" + str(humidity) +
"Pressure:" + str(pressure), scroll_speed=(0.08), back_colour= [0,0,200])
```

Ensure that all of the above code has been typed in a single line. The line will make the values for temperature, pressure and humidity scroll across the LED Matrix of Sense Hat.
We also need to ensure that the LED Matrix has been cleared once the script is killed for any reason. Add the following line at the script's bottom and after exception handling:

```
sense.clear()
```

Once the above changes have been made, you should end up with the following script:

```
#!/usr/bin/python
from sense_hat import SenseHat
import time
import sys

sense = SenseHat()
sense.clear()

try:
        while True:
                temp = sense.get_temperature()
                temp = round(temp, 1)
                print("Temperature C",temp)

                humidity = sense.get_humidity()
                humidity = round(humidity, 1)
                print("Humidity :",humidity)

                pressure = sense.get_pressure()
                pressure = round(pressure, 1)
                print("Pressure:",pressure)

                sense.show_message("Temperature C" + str(temp) \
                    + "Humidity:" + str(humidity) + "Pressure:" \
                    + str(pressure), scroll_speed=(0.08), back_colour= [0,0,200])

                time.sleep(1)
except KeyboardInterrupt:
        pass

sense.clear()
```

You can then press Ctrl + X, then Y, and hit the enter key. You will have saved and exited the script. Let us run it to test whether it is operating as expected by running the following command on the command prompt:

```
sudo python ~/weather_script.py
```

You will see the text begin to scroll across the LED matrix of the Sense Hat.

Using Initial State

Initial State is simply a website designed to be used for data storage as well as data analytics for IoT (Internet of things) devices like the Raspberry Pi. Open the website and sign up.

You just have to open the website, click on SIGN IN, then choose "Register A New Account".

Sign in to get an API key. Once the home page is open, look beneath "Streaming Access Keys" and find the "Create a New Key" button. Click the button and save the key.

We can then get the Python streamer for Initial State. The install script can be obtained directly from their website. The code can be viewed by opening the https://get.initialstate.com/python url on the browser. To enter the script, run the following command on the terminal:

```
curl -sSL https://get.initialstate.com/python -o - |
sudo bash
```

A prompt will be presented to you. Hit the N key to skip. Now that the streamer has been download, we can begin to edit the previous script. Open the script by running the following command on the terminal:

```
sudo nano ~/weather_script.py
```

A number of codes will have to be added to the script. Add the line given below to the file:

```
import sys
```

Followed by the following line:

```
from ISStreamer.Streamer import Streamer
```

What we have done is imported the Initial State streamer package. This will allow us to establish a connection to the website then stream our data to it. Add the following line:

```
logger = Streamer(bucket_name="Sense Hat Sensor Data",
access_key="YOUR_KEY_HERE")
```

Below the following line:

```
sense = SenseHat()
```

We will have created the streamer. Replace the:

```
print(
```

With the following:

```
logger.log(
```

At this point, your code should be as follows:

```
#!/usr/bin/python
from sense_hat import SenseHat
import time
import sys
from ISStreamer.Streamer import Streamer

sense = SenseHat()
logger = Streamer(bucket_name="Sense Hat Sensor Data", access_key="YOUR_KEY_HERE")
sense.clear()

try:
```

```
    while True:
        temp = sense.get_temperature()
        temp = round(temp, 1)
        logger.log("Temperature C",temp)

        humidity = sense.get_humidity()
        humidity = round(humidity, 1)
        logger.log("Humidity :",humidity)

        pressure = sense.get_pressure()
        pressure = round(pressure, 1)
        logger.log("Pressure:",pressure)

        time.sleep(1)
except KeyboardInterrupt:
    pass
```

Save the script and exit the editor. Run the following command on the terminal:

```
sudo python ~/weather_script.py
```

Data will be send to the website immediately. This can be seen on the left-hand side of the website page.

Conclusion

We have come to the end of this guide. You should now be able to implement projects in your Raspberry Pi 3 on your own.

You must have known how useful the Raspberry Pi is. The device can have different uses including home automation. For instance, you can use the raspberry Pi for home security. The Pi can be programmed using different programming languages. Examples include Python and Node.JS. With such programming languages, one can create complex and useful apps using the Pi. For beginners in computer programming, the Raspberry Pi is the best device to begin with. Other than computer programming, one can learn the basics of computer science with the device.

Thank you!

Thank you for buying this book. If you enjoyed reading this text and developing all the fun projects, then I'd like to ask you for a favor. **Would you be kind enough to leave a review on Amazon?**
It'd be greatly appreciated!

All my best wishes,

Steve